COLLECTION OF LIFE EXPERIENCES

By Precious Coker

ISBN Ebook: 978-1-972344-26-2

ISBN Paperback: 978-1-972344-27-9

ISBN Hardback: 978-1-972344-28-6

Editing & Interior Design by Silvestra Z. Griffin

Published by Parker Publishers

7345 W Sand Lake RD, STE 210 Office 3266 Orlando, FL 32819

Our books may be purchased in bulk for promotional, educational, or business use.

Please contact Parker Publishers at +1(689) 219-8883 or by email at contact@parkerpublishers.com

Printed in the United States.

Dedicated to the loving memory of my dearly beloved mother:
Mrs. Felicia Olueme Coker (Nee Imokhuede)

My late mother was an epitome of resilience, hard work and commitment to the success of her children.

Unfortunately for her, and due to circumstances beyond her control, she lived as and raised myself and three other siblings as a single mother even though her marriage was never annulled.

This book is to remember her, preserve her name and to encourage all women out there raising children as single mothers, it may be tough, seemingly thankless, but know this, by God's grace your children will turn out good.

My regret is that my mother never lived to enjoy the fruit of her tireless labor. I am pleased that right there in heaven, looking down she will be proud of the man she raised.

My dear Mummy, continue to rest in the bosom of the Almighty Lord, and light perpetual shine upon your gentle soul.

Preface

Collection Of Life Experiences is a story I have shared in bits with guests who, at one time or another, have visited with us.

It is about my journey, starting from when I was born in the university town of Zaria in Northern Nigeria. Somehow, the fortunes of my parents changed shortly after I was born, so I heard from grown-up whispers, but my mother always made me feel very special. She always praised my intellect, wisdom, poise, and demeanor, which I see summarized as: "Pre, a short form of my name Precious, you can live, stay, and co-exist anywhere with any type of persons."

When I realized all her efforts to survive and train us—her four surviving children, as two had passed on, an elder brother and a younger sister—I promised myself never to disappoint her.

When life's journey began, with its twists and turns, and I realized that there are many factors—beyond personal ability and intellect—that contribute to achieving one's goals at each milestone, I was taken aback by the manipulations occurring in the adult world.

When my mother passed away on November 30, 1979, my life kind of came to a halt. I lost my zeal and ambition for success. After all, I was working hard to make my mother proud; now she is gone.

When I decided to fill the emptiness of my life by starting my own family, I threw myself into ensuring my family is all in all to me. I still do today.

This book is in memory of my mother, Felicia Olueme Coker, who gave her all to ensure I not only survived, but excelled in my journey of life.

This story highlights actual real-life obstacles that, in African parlance, are referred to as "home trouble," which dogged every one of my moves to succeed in life.

My strong belief in God and the power of prayers made it possible for me to free myself and my family from all the vicissitudes of life, and to arrive at our promised land, Canada.

For all those who are downcast, believing that it is too late for them to succeed, or too late to make very bold moves to change their station in life, this book is for you. Read it and be motivated.

For those of you still holding on to pain and the loss of a loved one, read this book and draw inspiration, and the need to find a greater purpose in life to fill that void.

TABLE OF CONTENTS

COLLECTION OF LIFE EXPERIENCES

GROWING UP DAYS

Growing up in a town such as Zaria, a quiet university town in northern Nigeria, is quite an experience. The town itself is divided into districts or quarters. Zaria city is the heartland, surrounded by the famed Zaria wall—a city once defended by great warriors, including Queen Amina. Zaria City houses the Emir of Zazzau (Emir of Zaria). Inhabitants are predominantly Muslims, many of whom are palace workers, local government employees, or people who travel daily to work in Tudun Wada's hospital or Sabon Gari's government offices.

Tudun Wada, the district where the General Hospital is located, is where I was born. Before the civil war of 1967 and into the late 1970s, it was a first-class hospital where treatment, including prescription drugs, was free. Doctors, nurses, and pharmacists were well-trained and carried out their duties professionally.

Kongo, a section of Tudun Wada, hosts the Kongo campus of Ahmadu Bello University, with faculties of Law, Accounting, Business Administration, and other arts disciplines. It also has the Shagalinku Restaurant, which serves both Hausa and European cuisines. One could dine at a table or sit cross-legged on a mat to enjoy a bowl of "tuwo da miya dege-dege spiced with mai shanu."

Sabon Gari, where I spent the first twenty-three years of my life, was home to Igbos, Yoruba, Calabaris, Hausas, Fulanis, and many other tribes. Until the January 15, 1966 coup, little attention was paid to tribe or origin—people simply lived side by side. Christians, Muslims, and practitioners of African traditional religions shared the same space in harmony.

Other districts also stood out. Gaskiya was known for publishing "Gaskiya ta fi kobo (kwabo)," meaning "the truth is more valuable than a penny." It was the only Hausa newspaper in Nigeria at that time and also the site of Barewa College, which produced almost all the notable Northern Nigerian leaders, military and civilian.

Wusasa was home to St. Bartholomew's Anglican Church, the oldest Anglican church in Northern Nigeria, as well as its day and boarding primary school, also a first in the region. Across the railway tracks from St. Bartholomew's stood St. Paul's College, another famous institution.

Sabon Gari also had the Junior and Senior railway quarters, the Nigerian Tobacco Company, and the road leading to the Government Reservation Area (GRA). GRA housed top civil servants, professionals, business leaders, and expatriates. I remember the famed Theresa Bowyer private primary school and St. Andrew's Anglican Church located there.

Further out was Samaru, down to Chika, a district on the way to Funtua in today's Katsina State. Samaru is home to the prestigious Ahmadu Bello University, while Chika houses its School of Agriculture, surrounded by vast farmland for agricultural research.

Growing up in Zaria was a privilege, a blessing in cultural diversity and liberal spirit.

In Sabon Gari, there was also "New Layout," where retired civil servants, especially from the railway and Post & Telecommunications, built their dream homes. Sabon Gari is my birthplace and I conveniently call it my hometown—I am a Sabon Gari Zaria boy.

I was one of four surviving children out of six. Father was a banker; mother a nurse, teacher, and later a trader. Growing up was strange without a father around, leaving my mother to struggle alone with four children.

I was delivered at the General Hospital in Tudun Wada and taken to our house on Hospital Road, Sabon Gari, as recorded on my birth certificate. Later we moved to a two-bedroom apartment on Lagos Street, also in Sabon Gari. Lagos Street was popular for its proximity to the main market, where mother ran two stalls: one for plates, dishes, and cutlery, and the other for large, colorful metal bowls often bought as wedding gifts for Hausa brides.

We, her children, called her Mama Efe, after our eldest sister. Friends and acquaintances knew her as Mama Dada, but in time, we simply called her "Mummy." There is only one mummy in this story, and she is my beloved mother.

To supplement her income, Mummy bought raw reeds of sponge plant, soaked and separated them by hand, then molded and sold them as sponge balls. She also prepared sponges in between serving her customers, which fetched her needed "loose change." At night, she brought out her Singer sewing machine to sew clothes for clients. Sometimes I heard her quiet sobs while she worked, weighed down by the struggle of providing for four children.

Father, once a promising banker, had started as a cashier with the British Bank for West Africa. By the age of twenty-four, he already owned a twenty-four-room property on Hospital Road. Yet, as I grew up, I barely saw him; he had relocated to Lagos. Mother traded to survive after sending him proceeds from the sale of family property and shares.

I often overheard stories of the lavish naming ceremony that my father held for me. It was said that soon after that celebration, fortunes turned, and our family's decline began. Whatever the truth, it was Mummy who bore the burden of feeding, clothing, and educating us.

The firstborn was a girl, followed by a boy with knotted hair, who died before I was born. Then came two more girls, one also with the "dada" hair. Then another girl before me, the youngest, also born with knotted (dada) hair.

My mother's daily routine was endless: tending her stalls, organizing after-school lessons, making sponges, preparing dinner, and finally sewing at night. That was when the weight of her struggles surfaced. I would hear her quiet sobs or her questions whispered into the silence: "Where did the family go wrong?"

The suitcase, a big leather portmanteau with metal clasps, served as more than just a container for clothes; it was mummy's makeshift safe, the one place where she carefully tucked away all her most important documents. Inside were papers she considered vital—deeds, receipts, letters, and what she described as proof of how our family's fortunes had crumbled. That suitcase, which she guarded with such seriousness, was stolen one night during a burglary. The thieves did not break into a distant storeroom or hidden corner; they came right into our apartment, into the small space that was our only home, and they took it.

When she discovered the loss, I remember her silence first, then her tears. Later, she gathered us children and explained in her calm but weary voice that everything she had saved for years to explain our story was gone. She had been keeping those documents, she said, not for herself, but for us. One day, when she felt we were old enough to understand, she intended to sit us down and tell us the full truth of what happened—how we became broke, how our father was gone, and how she was left to carry the burden of raising four children alone. That day never came. With the theft of that suitcase, all the written evidence she had collected vanished.

What remained were only fragments of stories, whispers, and the weight of unanswered questions. Mummy reminded us from time to time that she had once kept proof, but she no longer had the means to back her words. In her heart, I believe she thought she would still tell us everything when the moment was right, but fate was unkind. She did not live long enough to reveal her side of the story.

And so the real truth of what went wrong with our family—whether it was sudden misfortune, betrayal, or choices made—remains forever hidden. What we are left with is only her struggle, her tears at night, her resilience in the face of hardship, and the memory of a stolen suitcase that carried away not just documents but perhaps the key to understanding our past.

EARLY LEARNING

It was a bright Monday morning in January, the year I was five months short of my sixth birthday. I remember it clearly because at the time, no matter how hard I tried, I could not stretch either of my arms across my head to touch the opposite ear — the traditional test of readiness for primary school. The rule then was simple: to gain admission, a child must either have turned six at their last birthday or be able to touch an ear across the head. I was neither. My sixth birthday was still months away, and my little arms stubbornly refused to grow those few extra inches.

But I had been pestering Mummy endlessly. Every morning, I would follow other children on their way to school, dragging my bare feet on the dusty path and pleading, "Mummy, I want to go too!" After weeks of my nagging, she finally gave in. With her old sewing machine, she made me a neat khaki shirt and shorts — the uniform of St. George's Primary School, Sabon Gari, Zaria.

On that fateful morning, she entrusted me to a neighbor whose son was six months older — a boy proudly qualified to attend because his hand reached his ear with ease. The two of us set off on foot, trekking the long, lively road to school, our faces glowing with excitement and dust.

When we arrived, the new admissions were gathered in a corner of the assembly ground, told to line up and wait for the teachers in charge of registration. The air was filled with the sound of children reciting morning prayers. When the assembly and devotion ended, the school band began to play its marching tune — a signal for all pupils to file into their classrooms.

As the drums and trumpets echoed through the air, I was completely spellbound. The band commander, with his gleaming command staff, rolled and twirled it with such grace that I forgot where I was. Each toss into the air caught the sunlight, each spin matched the beat of the drums. Without thinking, I left the line of new pupils and joined the marching crowd, happily matching step for step with the older children, completely unaware that I had just enrolled myself into St. George's.

Our neighbor, who also happened to be our church choir master, was frantic when he discovered I had vanished. He ran from one class to another until he found me seated proudly among registered pupils, ready for lessons I wasn't yet qualified to take. By then, my adventure had become the talk of the registration panel.

The teachers looked through my documents, noting that I was still five months shy of six and that my hand could not touch my ear — a double disqualification. Yet, seeing me in full uniform, standing smartly during assembly and marching confidently into class, they smiled. My boldness, and perhaps my mother's effort, softened their hearts. After a brief consultation, they decided to admit me. That day, at five years and seven months old, I became a pupil of the prestigious St. George's Anglican Primary School, Sabon Gari, Zaria — and the youngest in my class.

St. George's was an affiliate of St. George's Church under the Anglican Communion of the Church of England. School fees were paid in pounds, shillings, and pence — the remnants of colonial order. At that time, our eldest sister had already completed her First School Leaving Certificate (FSLC) and was pursuing secretarial studies through Pitman's of London. My two other sisters were still in primary school, and we often trekked together. Sometimes, they would give me a piggyback ride on the way, especially when I pretended to be too tired or slightly "ill." It was my clever trick to ride in comfort while they laughed and complained.

Learning came easily to me. I listened attentively in class, devoured every reading material I could find, and knew that Mummy would reinforce my lessons in the evening. Her "lesson," as she called it, took place in one of her market stalls — the one with plates and cutlery, because it was less cluttered. She would set small wooden stools called *joko* in a circle, and there I sat with one or two of my friends. We studied arithmetic and English from the famous *Lacombe* and *Student's Companion* textbooks. Arithmetic lessons meant endless drills of addition, subtraction, multiplication, and the mighty BODMAS, while English sessions involved spelling contests and reading aloud.

When the lesson ended, Mummy would hand me a tray of freshly made sponges to sell. I would balance it on my head, calling out "So-so! So-so!" as I walked through the streets. I sold each piece with pride, knowing I was helping Mummy in my small way. Every evening, after I sold all my wares, she would reward me with a shiny three-pence *toro*

— that brass-colored, eight-sided coin that gleamed in the sunlight. To me, it was treasure.

With my *toro* in hand, I would dash off to the playground or a quiet side street to play football. After the game, the coin bought fried yams, *akara* (bean cake), or bits of fried cow tendon called *ishan*. My friends and I shared the snacks, laughing and recounting goals that never were.

Before sunset, I always hurried to Sabon Gari Market to help Mummy close her stalls or carry groceries home — peppers, onions, and sometimes meat for dinner. Those small errands became my daily duty, and I was proud to be useful.

Mummy was an exceptional cook, and my time in her kitchen shaped me. My family today still agrees that I inherited her culinary touch. My early involvement wasn't entirely voluntary — though I loved the aroma of food frying in groundnut oil, I was drafted as the "official taster." It was my job to taste for salt, pepper, and spice balance, and to test the tenderness of beef, chicken, or guinea fowl.

I was also the designated catcher of dinner. Whenever Mummy decided it was time for chicken or guinea fowl, she would call out, "Go and bring one!" and I would chase the birds across the yard until I caught one. I handled the slaughtering too, dipping the bird into hot water to loosen the feathers before plucking them clean.

We rarely ate chicken eggs; they were less tasty. What we ate were guinea-fowl eggs — richer and tastier, whether boiled or fried. Sunday mornings were always special. Mummy made omelets of diced onions, peppers, and tomatoes fried in golden groundnut oil — the real kind, freshly pressed from roasted nuts. The fragrance filled the house long before breakfast was served. She placed the omelet beside boiled yams, poured steaming Bournvita with Peak milk into enamel cups, and that was our Sunday treat — simple, hearty, and unforgettable.

One Sunday morning, Mummy decided to try something new. She said she had discovered a healthy way to fry our omelet. Instead of the usual sweet-smelling groundnut oil, she poured cod-liver oil into the frying pan. The smell that filled the house was strong and strange, but she was confident it was good for us. When breakfast was served, each of us took a bite, and in no time, all four children were throwing up in every direction. It was confusion everywhere. That was the first and last time Mummy experimented with cod-liver oil. Church was cancelled that day, and cod-liver oil was permanently banned from our kitchen.

Our Sunday routine remained the same after that. The morning omelet before church was always followed by white rice and stew with fried chicken or guinea fowl after church. In those days, chicken and guinea fowl were cheaper than beef in Zaria. Farmers came from the surrounding villages carrying large basket-like coops filled with birds for sale. They usually preferred to sell in groups of six, and by evening, they lowered the prices just to go back home empty-handed. That was when Mummy bought her birds — sometimes the coop itself came along with the deal.

Saturdays were divided according to what needed to be done. There was *Laundry Saturday*, which was more of a family outing than a chore. All dirty clothes were packed into large metal basins — the old ones that were no longer good for sale in the shop. We usually carried three basins: two for laundry and one for food items, the kerosene stove, and snacks. Laundry soap, "blue" for whitening, and water containers completed the load.

We then walked to the Nigerian Railways Junior Service Quarters, where one of our uncles from the Post and Telecommunications Department lived. How a P&T worker managed to get quarters in the railway compound was never clear to me, but there was running water there and an outdoor tap we could use freely. It was about a thirty-minute walk carrying all our supplies.

On arrival, laundry was divided. I washed my own clothes; my sisters handled theirs, Mummy's, and the household items — bedsheets, pillowcases, and curtains. Clean clothes were spread out in the sun, and white garments were treated with "blue." Mummy was very particular about how to prepare blue water. You put enough water in a basin, placed some blue powder in your palm, stirred it, then lifted your hand to the sky to check if the color matched. If it was too light or too dark, you adjusted it until it looked right. Only then were the white clothes soaked and swirled, wrung by hand, lapped smooth, and hung neatly with clips to dry. That was Mummy's rule, and she made sure everyone followed it.

Another weekend routine was *Sanitation Saturday*. We stayed home to clean every part of the apartment, carried mattresses outside for sun-drying, and sprayed every corner with Flit. When the original fumigant finished, Mummy replaced it with kerosene in the sprayer. She sprayed the entire house until the air was thick with the smell, saying it would chase away all the insects and bugs.

Then there was *Digestive System Sanitation Saturday*, the most dreaded of them all. Nobody escaped it. No visitors, no outings. On the Friday before, Mummy always added Epsom salt to her shopping list. Early Saturday morning, we lined up to drink a warm cup of the salty mixture. It worked fast — first came vomiting, then repeated runs to the latrine. The latrine had already been scrubbed with Izal or carbolic acid, leaving that sharp hospital smell in the air.

After the whole process, everyone felt weak and empty. By evening, Mummy would prepare a special dinner to make up for it — pounded yam with ogbono soup, full of bush meat and snail. We ate outside under the open sky, each with a bowl of cold water filled with ice cubes I fetched from the small store across the street. We used cups to scoop the chilled water and drank between mouthfuls.

Mummy made her pounded yam herself. She peeled the yams, cut them into pieces, boiled them till soft, and pounded them in a wooden mortar with a pestle. She kept adding pieces until the yam became smooth and stretchy. That was the signal that dinner was ready.

Pounded yam is scooped and molded into balls of good size. The molds are then wrapped with clean kitchen towels or large napkins, placed under a pillow in the bedroom, and covered to keep them warm. The covering preserves the heat and softness of the pounded yam. Pounded yam is best enjoyed when it is hot, smooth, and free of lumps.

When the meal was over, dishes were soaked for washing. We would then gather around Mummy for bedtime stories. Sometimes, our questions turned serious — we would ask about her relationship with Father and why things had changed for our family. Mummy always gave the same answer: "The time is not right. When it is, I will tell you everything." She would say she had proof in the form of newspaper clippings, receipts, and property documents — evidence that would explain how everything fell apart.

Oh, Mummy was deeply hurt. I don't think she ever recovered from the loss of her portmanteau and the documents she kept inside. About eight years later, she was gone from this world.

That burglary happened during the wake-keep of our landlord, who had recently passed away. He was a dignified man with taste — tall, light-skinned, and always neatly dressed. He had sent his eldest son and daughter to study in the United Kingdom, something rare in those days. Whenever I wandered to the back of the compound where his apartment was, I would find him sitting in his reclining wooden chair — a sturdy frame with a cloth seat that looked like a hammock but stood on four legs.

Each time, he would stop whatever he was doing and question me. "Young man," he would begin, "if you meet your father today, will you forgive him for leaving your mother to raise you all alone?" His voice was calm, but his eyes fixed on me so firmly that an answer other than the one he expected felt impossible. I always shook my head, meaning no. I was young but old enough to know that an injustice had been done to my mother, my sisters, and me. Still, I could not understand why he asked so often.

It has always felt strange that on the very night of his wake-keep — the night meant to honor him — Mummy's portmanteau of evidence disappeared. The burglary was reported at the local police station, and Mummy visited the nearby garbage dump many times afterward, praying that the thieves had thrown away the documents after taking what they wanted. She searched through piles of rubbish, hoping to find even one piece of the papers she had guarded so closely. But nothing ever turned up. The evidence was gone forever — buried in her memory, just as our landlord's body was buried in the earth.

Some evenings after dinner, I would ask Mummy for permission to go outside and play with my friends. We gathered under the streetlight between our building and the next. In those days, no one cared about who was Christian, Muslim, or traditional worshipper. We were all just children from Sabon Gari, from Zaria — nothing more, nothing less.

Our favorite game was *buttons.* We drew a circle in the sand, stood a few steps back, and drew a line to mark our positions. Each player took turns flicking a button — usually taken from old shirts — toward the circle. If it landed inside, you waited for the next player. If it fell short, others could aim to hit it and "eat" it by knocking it into the circle. Disagreements often followed, sometimes settled by shouting, sometimes by fists. Bloodied noses were not unusual. Those small fights taught lessons we didn't yet understand — that life, even among friends, could be unfair.

My first real lesson in life came in primary school. At the time, you could complete elementary education after six years if you gained admission into secondary school, or stay seven years to earn the First School Leaving Certificate (FSLC). I believed I was bright enough to enter secondary school after six years, and I had my eyes set on St. Paul's College, Wusasa, Zaria (SPC).

I took the common entrance examination in Primary Six, choosing SPC as my first choice. I was confident — Mummy had given me extra lessons in Arithmetic and English, and she trained me to memorize complex admission numbers that mixed letters and figures. I could recite them without a mistake. When the admission list came out, I ran eagerly to check, but my name wasn't there. The list was filled with the names of children from influential families. That was my first encounter with disappointment and the realities of how adults' decisions shaped our world.

Mummy, whom the community called *Mama Dada*, was small in stature but full of strength and determination. To us, she was the most courageous and compassionate person we would ever know. People called her "clever," meaning intelligent and quick-witted. I first heard that word used for her by one of her old classmates, a professor of Fine Arts at Ahmadu Bello University, Samaru campus.

We met him one morning while walking to her stall at the main market. He got out of his car, greeted Mummy with excitement, and then turned to me. "Do you know your mother was one of the cleverest in our class? We could hardly keep up with her," he said.

Mummy only smiled and told him not to exaggerate, though her smile gave her away. I knew already — she didn't need anyone to tell me that.

After the professor left for the market, Mummy turned to me and said, "I am not one to tell a child what to study, but my advice is that you must obtain a degree first. After that, you can decide if you want to become a professor or pursue another profession. It is important that you acquire at least an undergraduate degree; it will broaden your mind and teach you to think critically."

Her words, coming right after the professor's praise, confirmed my belief that Mummy was truly a clever and thoughtful woman. She was courageous, quietly raising her children with the little she earned through sweat, grit, and tears. The physical, spiritual, and mental well-being of her children was the reason she lived on despite the monumental tragedies and loss she had gone through.

She lost her first son, the accounts of which were never explained. Her last daughter, born after me, died under strange circumstances. On one of her trips between Zaria and Kano aboard the Nigerian Railway passenger train, she was traveling to look after my immediate elder sister, who had been admitted to the ECWA Eye Specialist Hospital in Kano after suddenly becoming blind in both eyes one fateful morning.

On her way back from one of these visits, she noticed that her youngest daughter, strapped to her back, had been sleeping for too long and might need feeding and a diaper change. She unstrapped the little girl, only to discover that she was stone cold dead. She pretended the baby was still alive, then later strapped her back on, sat quietly, suppressed a wail, and cried silently, lost in her thoughts. Only God knows what went through her mind at that moment.

When the train arrived at the Zaria station, she quietly walked home with a dead baby strapped to her back, another daughter left in the care of strangers at the eye clinic in Kano. She arrived home, broke the news to neighbors and the community, made preparations, and buried her last daughter.

I will never know whether these tragedies or some other incidents made Mummy resilient in protecting her children.

We lived in a compound with several neighbors. One couple, who lived in the front section where the wife ran a small food shop, were known to belong to a secret cult. They often returned from meetings late at night, sometimes at dawn. Because our apartment was closest to the gate, Mummy often had to unlock it for them. I once overheard her warning the couple that if any harm ever came to her or her children, she would not take it quietly.

To make daily life easier, Mummy arranged that the woman would keep the key to our apartment. If any of us returned early or needed to get in while Mummy was still at the market, we could collect the key from her.

One day, my immediate elder sister came home sick from school. She had travelled from Kaduna, about ninety kilometers away, by public transport. She collected the key from the neighbor, entered the house, and went straight to bed. Mummy only learned later in the evening that her daughter had returned ill. When she found out, she attended to her immediately, giving her medicine and comfort. Then she asked if the neighbor who gave her the key had come to check on the sick child. The answer was no.

Mummy went straight to the woman's shop and told her to stop what she was doing and follow her. She made her come and see the child she had given the key to, but had failed to check on. After the visit, Mummy warned her again —if any misfortune befell her children, she would hold them responsible.

We continued living in that compound for a few more years. The couple kept their position in their society, attending their secret meetings. Eventually, when my siblings and I were older, we moved to a better apartment.

Mummy was an active member of the Dorcas Society of St. George's Anglican Church, Sabon Gari, Zaria, where she served as the financial secretary. The Dorcas Society was not as flashy as the Lady Workers' Society, which had younger, fashion-conscious women who dressed elegantly to church. Dorcas members were mostly middle-aged and elderly women, committed to service rather than appearance.

Their activities included fundraising, collecting gently used clothing for orphanages, homes for the elderly, and the leprosy settlement in Sayi, near Zaria. Members also adopted elderly women who had no families. The adopted elder became their "mother," and the member was responsible for her welfare, working with the church's welfare department to meet her needs.

Mummy adopted Mrs. Taylor, the wife of Jonnie Taylor, a Sierra Leonean who had settled in Zaria. Everyone called her *Mamie Saro*. She became our adopted grandmother. By then, she had lost all her family but still spoke fondly of her late husband, Jonnie, recalling their life together with joy and always with a glint in her eyes.

Mummy was involved in almost all volunteer jobs in the church. She was a member of the Parochial Church Committee (PCC); this committee is the think-tank of the church. She was also a member of the harvest committee and many others. She attended early morning Holy Communion services, Sunday services, and weekly evening services. She dedicated her life to the service of God. She was also a community servant, associated with the Bendel Women's Society, a cultural society of women from the Benin-Delta area of Nigeria resident in Zaria. She was also the financial secretary of the Owan Women's Society, a cultural group of women from the Owan district of the then Bendel State.

Mummy was actively involved in all activities concerning the welfare of traders in the Sabon Gari Zaria main market. She spoke English, Hausa, Yoruba, and Ora fluently and was an excellent communicator in all four languages.

Mummy loved visiting members of her societies — both church and cultural — and she always went with gifts. She was happiest when she heard that a member's child had gained admission into secondary school and was headed for the boarding house. She knew exactly what the admission list required, especially the hardware. Mummy would gather items from her stall, such as buckets, plates, and cutlery, to present as gifts — her contribution to the new boarding student. She was very generous and blessed with a giving heart.

MY PHOBIA FOR SWIMMING

In life, there are certain events that leave indelible marks on one's mind and memory — things that shape behavior, attitude, and sometimes even phobia. Growing up in Sabon Gari, Zaria, there was a "river" called Kogi. Kogi was not a myth, but rather a place known for mysterious and tragic occurrences.

Almost every year, one child — some family's son — was lost to the Kogi River. It was a body of flowing water far from central Sabon Gari, surrounded by farmlands. During the rainy season, when schools were on break, pupils and students on holiday would go to the farms to enjoy "free" fruits and sugarcane without permission. Afterward, they would take turns diving into Kogi, laughing and splashing. Sometimes the cheerful laughter would suddenly stop — someone was drowning. Fishermen or farmers might rescue one, or the body of another would be pulled out later. "Kogi has taken another one," people would say, sighing and shaking their heads.

Most of those who drowned did not know how to swim. They joined others because of peer pressure or fear of being mocked. Every time such sad news spread through Sabon Gari, people would acknowledge it the same way: *Kogi has done its thing again.*

For this reason, once schools went on vacation, every household in Sabon Gari warned their sons. Mummy would plead with me, reminding me of the past deaths, and say she could never bear to lose me, not to carelessness. To her, drowning in Kogi was pure carelessness. I cannot recall how many times she gave me that stern warning, but I remember that I never went near Kogi. That is how effective Mummy's warnings and subtle threats were. Very effective.

Now, what was the event that left an indelible mark on me and shaped my fear of streams, rivers, seas, oceans, and even swimming pools?

I must have been around seven years old, hanging around boys two or more years older than I was. One Saturday morning — a Saturday that was neither laundry day nor digestive system sanitation day in our house — I had plenty of free time. I decided to join a band of boys aged between seven and ten.

Our plan that Saturday morning was to go on an adventurous walk through the Nigerian Railway Junior Service Quarters and on to the Senior Service Quarters.

Lining the way were mango trees heavy with ripe fruit of every variety and species. There were the bean-shaped ones with nipple-like tips called *opioro*, best eaten by squeezing from the base to the tip to push the juice upward, then biting the tip and sucking the juice out. That was everyone's favorite. I preferred the large species, best eaten sliced with a penknife. We all carried the *Okapi* brand penknife.

There were also the "kerosene" mangoes, so called because they gave off a kerosene smell — like the fuel used in lamps and cooking stoves.

After eating our fill from the different varieties — most of which we brought down with sticks and stones — one of the older boys, in a burst of adventure, shimmied up a mango tree and shook the branches so that ripe fruits came down in a shower. We picked as many as we could.

When we had eaten enough, one of the older boys suggested we go further and walk along the railway lines toward Wusasa. After walking several kilometers, we came to a bridge. Under the bridge was a river, not Kogi.

Farmers had cultivated sugarcane all around the area. The tall stalks looked inviting. We sat by the riverbank beneath the bridge and helped ourselves. We pulled out the long sugarcane stems, scraped them clean with our penknives, broke them at the nodes, peeled off the outer layer, and sucked on the fibrous cane until it was dry.

Sucking sugarcane is addictive; you can go on for hours, unaware of your surroundings or the time. We had our fill of free sugarcane taken from a farm we didn't own and hadn't sought permission to enter. Then came the reckless suggestion — one of the mischievous older boys proposed that we go for a swim in the river under the bridge.

I knew I was reminded in my mind of the evils of Kogi. This was not Kogi after all; this was under the railway bridge, far away from Kogi and its murderous tendencies. All the cautionary advice and pep talks about the dangers of swimming in open rivers were pushed to the back recesses of my mind. I could barely hear Mummy's warnings and her sometimes subtle threats.

I threw all caution to the wind, took off my clothes, and dived into the icy-cold water just as I had seen the "bigger" boys doing. Diving into the cold water is all I remember. When I came to, a few of us younger boys had just been rescued by farmers who heard our friends' cries for help.

Copious amounts of water were squeezed out of us. I was drained, tired, red-eyed, and pale. We rested while the farmers praised God that they were able to rescue us with no fatalities.

As they say, bad news travels fast. An embellished version had already spread all over Sabon Gari. The story was that a group of boys had drowned in the river under the railway bridge. Parents were already searching for their children, and I was mentioned as one of the boys involved.

When we finally gathered the courage to head back home, completely sober and ashamed, we marched into town with red eyes and dry, white skins. People stared at us in surprise, whispering as we passed.

I got home in one piece despite the wild stares and murmurs from onlookers. Looking at the faces of my two sisters, I knew that I was "done for." That was our term for saying one's goose was cooked — meaning the trouble ahead was serious.

Mummy returned from her evening church engagement — it might have been a meeting or service, I can't recall. She looked straight into my eyes without saying a word. That was all the message I needed; my goose was truly cooked.

I had dinner in silence. I could neither join my sisters' conversation nor go out to play with my friends under the streetlights. I went to bed early with the heavy feeling that my troubles were only beginning. Mummy's cold stare and loud silence were more frightening than any shouting could have been.

In the middle of my sleep, sometime before dawn, I felt a tap, then another, followed by Mummy's voice — heavy with sorrow and disappointment — asking if I wanted to send her to an early grave with my selfish and thoughtless behavior.

Before I could respond, a barrage of strokes from her two-edged cowhide whip landed on my legs. I jumped up in pain, trying to dodge each strike as she whipped my feet. The flogging continued as I cried, begged, and shouted promises that I would never again go near any body of water, let alone attempt to swim.

This tapping, waking me at dawn, and whipping my legs continued for a full week — every day, at the same time. Each time, I repeated my promise and declaration never to go near a river or swimming pool.

You know how certain events can make someone develop a phobia or lose interest in something entirely? Those early-morning whippings erased every thought of swimming from my mind. I developed a fear of water — rivers, lakes, even swimming pools.

My wife had a similar experience in her own childhood, though under different circumstances and in a different town. Her story and mine are good examples of how certain experiences can leave lasting marks on one's mind and shape behavior, attitude, and fears.

Now that we have our own children, neither of us can swim. We never registered them for swimming classes or encouraged them to swim. There are no swimmers in our home. Our children, however, are trying to correct that. They have enrolled their own children — our grandchildren — in swimming lessons.

I am grateful for the way I was raised. We were taught that if you spare the rod, you spoil the child. We believed in community upbringing — neighbors always looked out for one another and for the children. Corporal punishment was normal in schools, at home, and even during choir practice in church. Smacking an erring child was not seen as cruelty; it was discipline.

You couldn't be caught in the wrong place at the wrong time without being scolded or smacked by an adult, who would then report you to your parents. Growing up, I remember clearly that people genuinely looked out for one another.

SECONDARY SCHOOL DAYS

After completing Primary Seven and sitting for that year's common entrance, I again chose St. Paul's College, Wusasa, Zaria, as my first choice. This time, my name was on the admissions list. I was very excited.

Before the St. Paul's list was published, other schools such as St. John's College, Kaduna, Barewa College, Zaria, Commercial College, Zaria (a private vocational college), Government Secondary School, Zaria, and Government College, Kaduna, had already released theirs. Many of my friends found their names on those lists. I waited with bated breath. Deep down, I was confident that when the St. Paul's list was published, my name would be there. Mummy wondered, but she shared in my optimism. When the list finally came out, my name was on it — I was headed to St. Paul's College, Wusasa, Zaria.

My sisters were equally excited about my admission to the prestigious St. Paul's College. My two older sisters swung into action, buying pure white cotton fabric to sew sets of bed sheets and pillowcases. They were creative enough to knit my name along the edges of each set. With Mummy's permission, items from her shop that appeared on my provision list were set aside for me. My sisters went to great lengths to label all my items, either by knitting or by painting my name for easy identification.

After all the preparations, I advised against including food items such as beverages, powdered milk, Bournvita, Milo, sugar, condensed milk, or sardines. I preferred a small sack of *garri* (cassava flakes), fried beef, sugar, and coconut. My dear sisters, however, insisted that my list of provisions must look complete — after all, their younger brother was going to St. Paul's College, Wusasa, Zaria.

On the first day of school, Mummy's friend — her former neighbor in Kaduna before I was born — now the wife of the newly ordained Archdeacon of the Church of England (Anglican Communion), St. George's Anglican Church, Zaria, came with her driver to take me to school in their gleaming Peugeot 403 saloon car.

I sat in front with the driver while Mummy and her friend sat at the back. We arrived at St. Paul's College, Wusasa, Zaria, passing through the only main street in Wusasa where one could see the grounds of St. Luke's Anglican Hospital, the General Park and Market, St. Bartholomew's Church — the oldest Anglican Church in Northern Nigeria — and the cemetery beside it.

Driving further into Wusasa, we passed St. Francis of Assisi College of Theology and, on the same road from Sabon Gari, St. Bartholomew's Anglican School, popularly known as St. Barts.

Seeing all these historic landmarks in Wusasa made my first trip to boarding school very memorable. After crossing the railway line separating St. Barts from St. Paul's, we arrived at the grounds of the almighty SPC, Wusasa, Zaria.

The driver took us straight to Crowther House, located close to the principal's residence.

I alighted and retrieved my belongings, which included a hoe, a cutlass, and a metal bucket in addition to my box — commonly called a "coffin," made of metal and built to withstand rough handling. We were welcomed by prefects selected for the occasion and a few senior students eager to display their authority.

After the goodbyes and a warm embrace from Mummy and her generous friend, who had ensured that I arrived at school in a dignified manner, I watched as the driver pulled away. Mummy kept glancing back through the car window, waving until they were out of sight.

The lurking Form Two students pounced on me; this was what they did to every new student. They introduced themselves and made sure you repeated their names with the prefix *Senior*.

In St. Paul's College, every student is called by their surname. You must remember to prefix the names with *Senior* if they are a class or more above you.

I was shown to my section of the house. This section was a collection of 6" by 2½' metal double bunk beds arranged side by side, with about a 1½' spacing between them. Mattresses could be made of foam or of straw and cotton; each student provided his own mattress to fit the bed.

At the four corners of each section of the dormitory (or house) were closed-off cubicles, created using wooden poles tied to the foot of single beds and enclosed with bedsheets or printed African fabric. The enclosure had a partition between the sheets, often held in place with clothes pegs to secure the entrance. These cubicles provided privacy for their occupants, usually prefects or final-year students.

Each section had a mix of double and single bunks occupied by students from Forms One to Five. Upper and Lower Six students were housed in cubicles demarcated by cement block walls attached on both sides of the dormitory.

My first encounter with bullying in boarding school came from a group of Form Two students in my dormitory. They thought I was arrogant and cocky. One of their classmates had been my classmate in Primary Six at St. George's Primary School. He was one of the two who left for St. Paul's College from St. George's that year. His classmates knew that we had known each other from primary school and decided to help him assert his authority as a senior in St. Paul's College.

They would rile me, sending me on all kinds of crazy errands. I was fed up and decided to stand up for myself. I took on the ringleader of this group of Form Two boys from Crowther House who had been making my life difficult. I grabbed him by the legs, lifted him, and slammed him on the floor, rained a few blows on him, and ran for my dear life.

I only returned to my dormitory after "lights out". I got into my bed fully dressed, with my mosquito net still up instead of tucked in, giving the mosquitoes free access to feast on me all night.

The next morning, I was awake before the dormitory alarm signaled *rise and shine*. Everyone, at the sound of the alarm, went to their assigned areas for morning chores. Morning chores included sweeping the dormitory floors, washing latrines, or tending flower beds. Washing the latrines was usually reserved for first form students.

As soon as I got up, I dressed in my uniform, still wearing a shirt and shorts underneath, which made my dressing look stiff and awkward. I ran away from the dormitory to the classroom area. I had been warned the day before that, after my incident with the Form Two boys, they were looking for a way to deal seriously with me.

The "hide and seek" with this vengeance-seeking group continued for about three days—days in which I neither took a bath nor changed my clothes. My unkempt look caught the attention of one of the teachers, who remarked that I looked like a locomotive driver.

Some senior boys in our dormitory got wind of my situation, decided to broker peace, and called for a truce. The result of their intervention was that I would serve two hours of detention each day for two days. My punishment was to clear a section around the dormitory overrun by weeds and tall grass.

I served my two days of detention and tried to return to normal life—brushing my teeth, taking regular baths, and obeying dormitory rules. Whenever I came across the Form Two boys, they would still try to poke me, jab me, or give me a dirty look. I generally ignored them and went on my way.

The effects of those nights without a mosquito net soon showed up in the form of fever, chills, shivering, and a high temperature. The diagnosis was malaria — a serious bout of it. Malaria was a common ailment at home while growing up; we never slept under mosquito nets. But in the dormitory, sleeping under a net greatly reduced mosquito bites and malaria attacks.

I took a trip to the school dispensary for first-aid treatment and was subsequently referred to the General Hospital in Tudun Wada.

When I was growing up, I never noticed Mummy being ill to the extent of visiting the hospital, let alone being admitted. Whenever she felt under the weather or tired, she would attribute the condition to the onset of malaria or just general body weakness due to fatigue.

If she began to feel that way while at her stalls in the market, she would send me home to prepare a drink that would ease the symptoms and help her relax.

I would return home from the market, go to pluck some *neem* leaves (*dogon-yaro* leaves) from the *dogon-yaro* trees growing in the yards of both our old church and the site of the proposed new church building. After collecting the leaves, I rinsed them properly and squeezed them to extract the green, very bitter juice.

As soon as Mummy returned from the market, she would give me money to go across the street to the "off" and "on" liquor-licensed store to buy a small bottle of stout — the black alcoholic beverage produced by Guinness

Breweries. I would then mix for her a drink made of half *dogon-yaro* juice and half stout.

Mummy would relax with this mixture, and as soon as she finished the last sip, she would fall into a deep, restful sleep. She always slept soundly whenever she took this mixture. There was always some stout left in the bottle after preparing her drink, and I would finish whatever remained.

Mummy's stout and *dogon-yaro* mixture always seemed to work for her. She said it helped her sleep and prevented malaria symptoms from developing into full malaria illness. I believed her, and I always looked forward to preparing the mixture — it guaranteed that I got to finish what was left in the bottle.

In addition to making the simple *dogon-yaro* and stout mixture, I also learned the art of preparing a herbal mixture popularly called *agbo.*

This *agbo* recipe included mango tree bark, dried papaya and hibiscus leaves, fresh mango, lemon, and orange leaves, lemongrass, and slices of orange and lemon. All of these ingredients were placed in a large earthenware pot. Water was added, and the pot was set on a tripod. Firewood was pushed between the tripod legs and lit. The pot was left to boil for a long time.

By this time, the boiling had extracted the juices and essence from everything in the pot. A cup or two of the very dark brown liquid — *agbo* — would be drawn and set aside to cool. The remaining liquid was poured into a bucket. Whoever showed severe symptoms of malaria would then be covered with blankets, with their face placed close to the steam rising from the bucket. They were instructed to inhale and exhale deeply, breathing in the steam.

Within minutes, the person would be drenched in sweat. The remaining concoction in the bucket was then diluted with water until it reached a temperature suitable for bathing. The person was instructed to take a quick shower with the mixture.

After bathing with the *agbo* extract mixed with water, the *agbo* that had been set aside earlier would by then be cool enough to drink. This steaming, bathing, and drinking treatment was known to be a very good remedy for curing malaria symptoms.

I enjoyed every time I took part in steaming, bathing, and drinking *agbo*. Drinking Mummy's *dogon-yaro* and stout mixture, and later the *agbo* concoction, made my tongue familiar with bitter-tasting beverages.

Finishing the remaining stout after preparing Mummy's *dogon-yaro* mixture encouraged the early development of a taste for alcoholic beverages in me.

At St. Paul's College, every fortnight we usually had what was called "Outing Day." After the Saturday morning deep cleaning of the dormitories, latrines, and flower beds, each of the six houses would be inspected by a team made up of teaching staff, the vice principal, and the principal.

A team of two or three inspectors was assigned to each house. Points were deducted for infractions as the team walked through their assigned dormitory. Housekeeping infractions ranged from unironed bedsheets and uniforms, poorly made beds, to unpleasant odors from the latrines.

Any student whose carelessness caused deductions from their house's total points was given detention hours equal to the marks lost. Detention on "no-outing" weekends did not hurt as much, but detention on "outing" weekends was a real punishment. It meant you were grounded and could not visit Wusasa, Tudun Wada, or Sabon Gari for your usual out-of-school fun.

All students tried to be on their best behavior around teachers, school and house prefects, and senior students during the week leading up to "outing" Saturday.

Students also did their best to avoid "wall ironing" their white bedsheets, especially before inspections on outing days. Wall ironing was when, after washing, the bedsheet was left dripping wet and plastered against the smooth, oil-painted bathroom wall. It was then carefully spread flat so the water could drain evenly. The dry Samaru air ensured the sheet dried fast and smooth on the wall.

Once dry, the sheets were removed, neatly folded, and kept ready to be spread on beds on inspection day. A lazier method was to fold the bedsheet, spread it on cardboard placed between the mattress and bedspring, and sleep on it for a few days so it would appear ironed.

A group of friends from different houses and I somehow discovered that we had all tasted alcohol in one way or another, and a small bond gradually formed between us. Some members of this group had developed a habit of smuggling a few bottles of high-priced spirits from their fathers' cellars at home, managing to escape scrutiny both there and at school.

These bottles were hidden in a spot outside the school fence, and a couple would be retrieved on "Outing Day." Even though my home was in Sabon Gari, I didn't always visit on outing Saturdays. When I did, I stayed as long as possible before dashing off to meet my friends.

We normally kept our pocket money with our housemasters. Every Saturday after inspection, the housemaster brought out a notebook to record whatever amount each student requested and received from their savings

Collecting our money kept with the housemaster for safekeeping and monitoring our spending habits felt like an invasion of privacy. I devised a way to avoid suspicion about my spending. I always asked for just enough for transport to and from Sabon Gari from our housemaster. He liked my "prudence" and would always cite me as a good example of a responsible student who understood the value and use of money.

I had a well-kept secret: I stashed most of my pocket money taped to the inside of my luggage. The inside of my metal "suitcase," popularly called a "coffin," was lined with old newspaper held in place with Scotch tape. A carefully cut portion allowed access to the paper lining to deposit or retrieve notes.

After we had all collected pocket money from our various housemasters, we met at a point near the rail line leading out of the school boundary. From there, we began the long walk to Wusasa's main market to catch a bus to Sabon Gari.

Some of the money went on new comics for the comic buffs, some on a decent lunch, and some was added to a common purse reserved for our usual visits to a bar for relaxation and drinks. That was the highlight of our "outing Saturday." In the bar, we mixed hard liquor with beer for maximum effect. We always carried at least two bottles of hard liquor, retrieved from our stash hidden behind the school fence.

Some of us held our drink well even at an early age; others struggled. We always made sure every one of us got back to school before curfew and stayed out of trouble with the authorities.

Throughout the following days of the new week, we usually found time to gather and rehash our individual experiences of the last "Outing Saturday" and make plans for the next one.

An event happened in the very first week of our resumption into Form One at St. Paul's College, Wusasa, Zaria. This event eventually came to be known as "Como," derived from the English word *commotion*. Como was actually a riot that broke out, sending the whole school into lockdown. The principal had to invite a batch of police officers in anti-riot gear to the school to restore order.

There had been underlying animosity between the Fifth Formers on one hand and the Sixth Formers (Upper and Lower Six) on the other. Prefects were normally selected from the ranks of the Sixth Formers to allow the Fifth

Formers to concentrate on preparing for their final exams —
the West African School Certificate.

The Fifth Formers wanted nothing to do with the Sixth
Formers trying to exercise "seniority" over them by
enforcing discipline. They considered themselves beyond
the control of the Sixth Formers.

Among the students were some Fourth Formers who
were repeating a year; if they had passed their promotion
exams, they would have been in Fifth Form. Some of these
repeaters were well-built, heavyset boys who sided with
their friends now in Fifth Form. They too refused to accept
the authority of the Sixth Formers.

As with everything that is explosive, it only needed a
spark for an explosion to occur.

Dinner was normally served around 7:00 p.m. every
evening. On that fateful evening, while we new intakes were
still learning "table manners" and how to serve at our allotted
dining table, a prefect from Sixth Form was making an
announcement from the middle of the dining hall.

Service at dinner included bringing a salt cellar, fetching
water in a large aluminum kettle to be poured for all
members of a table — at least ten students.

While the prefect was speaking, a repeating Fourth
Former — acting as planned by members of the current Fifth
Form — confronted him in the middle of his announcement.
There was an exchange of words, voices were raised, and
fingers pointed in both directions. The entire dining hall's
attention shifted to the commotion in the center.

Then, as if on cue, from different corners of the hall, a Fifth Former or a repeating Fourth Former could be seen confronting any Sixth Former in sight. The confrontation quickly degenerated into physical fighting on all sides. Chairs and tables became missiles, and plates of food flew across the hall.

We were young, confused and afraid. Some of us attached ourselves to a band of senior students and headed for the legendary Kufena rock behind our school. The trek was a bit long and tortuous; it was dark, journey was unplanned, and we had made no preparations.

From our hide-out far away, we observed the red and blue flashing police lights confirming the presence of authorities who had come to quell the "Como".

A while later — could be one or four hours — I was too confused to keep track of time. Word eventually reached those of us who had taken refuge in the hills of Kufena to come down and return to school. No one slept that night.

At the school assembly the next day, the principal, in his usual dramatic fashion, described in vivid detail what had been reported to him and what he had personally witnessed during the previous night's chaos. He reminded us all of the presence of the Nigerian Police Force.

He declared that the Fifth Formers were suspended for the rest of their stay in the school. They would return only as day students to write their final examination — the West African School Certificate Examination — under police escort.

They were individually marched with the police to their dormitories to retrieve their belongings and vacate the school premises immediately. The complicit repeating Fourth Formers received the same treatment.

That event remained indelible in the minds of all First Formers. I know for certain that it shaped my perspective of boarding-house life and the concept of seniority as practiced at St. Paul's College, Wusasa, Zaria. The exercise of seniority was serious business.

I cannot recall how it began — maybe it was the invitation of the great Pelé and his team, Santos of Brazil, on their playing tour of Nigeria. Pelé and his team were invited to play a match at the Ahmadu Bello Stadium in Kaduna.

Our group just knew that we had to be in that stadium to see the legendary Pelé play. We decided to extend our escapades beyond the boundaries of Zaria and go "inter-city."

A member of our "Outing Saturday" group told us that he had a brother working in Kaduna and living in a one-room apartment. The brother would be out of town the weekend of Pelé's visit and had given us permission to use the apartment.

That Saturday was not even our official outing day. We gathered our money, dressed in our uniforms, skipped school after the morning inspection, and headed for Kaduna by public transport — about six of us in total.

We paid the student gate fee to enter the stadium, still wearing our school uniforms. After the football match, we went to the borrowed apartment, bought food from street vendors, and stocked up on enough beer and some hard liquor retrieved from our stash back at school.

The next day, Sunday, was visiting day at two popular girls' secondary schools in Kaduna — St. Faith's Anglican Girls' School, Kawo-Kaduna, and Queen of Apostles Catholic Girls' College, Kaduna South.

The obvious choice for our visit was Queen of Apostles, because the "loud-mouth" of our group had sisters attending that school. We all agreed that there were real "lookers" in Queen of Apostles and that their school uniform brought out the best of their beauty.

Off we headed to Queen Amina, gaining access to the visiting ground through the visiting pass provided by our friend's sisters.

Just being in an area filled with all those beautiful damsels — most of them strutting about with flirtatious looks and the proud carriage of peacocks — we ogled, stared, and imagined things. One of us was going out with one of the sisters of our loud-mouthed friend. They were lovers then and remained so for a long time.

When we were done staring, it was time to say our goodbyes and head "home" to school. We took our leave and went to the nearest motor park to board a bus back to Zaria.

We dropped off at the by-pass that allowed us to board another bus to Wusasa. By then, we had changed from our "outing" uniform of white shirt over white shorts to our "dorm" uniform of khaki shirt over khaki shorts.

Avoiding the main Wusasa road that led to the school — the one passing in front of St. Bartholomew's Church, St. Luke's Hospital, and Pa Gowon's house, the home of the father of Nigeria's then Head of State and Commander-in-Chief of the Armed Forces — we took a different route.

We navigated our way through farmlands, using the tall maize stalks and other foliage as cover, passing through the area around "Lovers' Rock," a hill easy to climb and perfect for a picnic or to relax and listen to music during "Outing Saturdays" for students who didn't go to Sabon Gari, Tudun Wada, or Kongo on such weekends.

Breaking out of the farmlands, we crossed the railway line and crawled under the surrounding barbed-wire fence into another maize plantation near one of the dormitories named Kalejaiye House.

From this hideout in the maize plants, we left the polythene bags containing our "outing" uniforms and other belongings used on the trip under some foliage, to be retrieved later. We did this so we could easily blend into the general school population in our khakis, pretending we had been in school all the while.

Our pretense did not work. We had missed one "lights out" and several roll calls. Prefects in our individual houses were on the lookout for us. They quickly figured out that we might have gone to Kaduna to see the famous footballer, Pelé — and they were right.

We were all given one week's detention. Detention was held after classes and lunch; we missed both siesta and games time. Our task was to create a new dumpster and incinerator by digging a six-foot-by-six-foot square hole, six feet deep. This new project was to be located behind each of our dormitories. When completed, the hole would serve as the new dumpster, where garbage from the dormitories would be thrown and periodically set on fire.

When the hole eventually became full, composted, and pressed down, other students would cover it with dirt, and a new hole would be started by the next unfortunate group of students who committed an offence serious enough to earn such punishment.

We toiled for a whole week, missing our siesta and games time. We had no regrets — I had no regrets.

I am not sure if it was this trip or another of our "outings" when I first noticed that some members of our group had picked up the habit of cigarette smoking. I did not start smoking cigarettes until my final year at St. Paul's College.

Later, the group also noticed that one of our members had developed the habit of smoking weed — which we called *Indian Hemp* — in addition to cigarettes. He was the only one among us who did so, but he never smoked weed around us. He did that with a different group from his hostel, Mort House.

Mort House was close to the non-teaching staff quarters, near one of the back gates of the school that led to Wusasa village. It was easy for students from this dormitory, Mort House, to access the village for all sorts of purchases, including *Indian Hemp* and cigarettes.

This member of our group later in life retired as a Brigadier General in the Nigerian Army.

Throughout my time in Crowther House, up to the end of my fourth year, neither my seniors nor my juniors knew that I was one of the best students academically in my class. After class activities, my behavior and disposition created the impression that I was not academically serious. I was always in the company of our group members, most of whom were, at best, average students.

I had promised myself that Mummy's sacrifices to ensure I obtained the best education would not be in vain. I made sure that every new school year, I secured the first seat in every classroom I was assigned to. Sitting in front guaranteed that I could see the blackboard clearly, hear the teacher properly, and stay less involved in horseplay or chattering — what we called "noise making."

I listened in class, took extra notes from what teachers dictated, and spent most of my free periods — times not assigned to any subject — in the school library.

I always did well in my studies. I was a science student with a flair for literature. In my fourth year, I registered for English Literature in addition to my core science subjects — Physics, Chemistry, and Biology.

My Fourth Form Biology teacher was, at that time, also the House Master for Crowther House, my dormitory.

We completed our promotion exams for the final year and had one week before vacation. That week was used by teachers to grade the exams and prepare report cards for students to take home to their parents.

The biology examination consisted of written theory questions, a practical exam, and a multiple-choice test called "objective." I was one of the best Biology students in my set — and that year, in the promotion examination, I was the best.

My attitude in the dormitory and after class did not qualify me to be considered for a "junior prefect" position, the usual stepping stone to becoming a full prefect. Prefects held leadership positions in the dormitory and classroom areas.

Prefects were chosen based on the recommendations of outgoing prefects, housemasters, and subject teachers. Students were observed, and notes were taken on their leadership qualities and general disposition. I was never considered as an understudy.

After our housemaster — my Fourth Form Biology teacher — had marked our biology scripts (theory, practical, and objective test papers), he left the marked scripts in a cardboard box we called a "carton."

Some outgoing seniors and prefects from my house, Crowther House, were invited to carry out certain chores for the biology teacher. One of these tasks involved properly sorting the three scripts — theory, practical, and objective — of each student and collating them accordingly.

This exercise gave them the opportunity to see the performances of all Fourth Form Biology students. They were shocked by my scores. Each of them later told me so individually after returning from their assignment in the housemaster's home.

On their return, I was called aside separately by each of the Fifth Formers who had seen my biology exam results — the highest that year. The question they all asked was the same: "Do we have another student in this school bearing the same name as you?"

I replied, "No, why?" They told me about their work at the biology teacher's house and how they came across my scores. I simply said, "Those are my scores, and that's what it normally will be."

They were very impressed. For the rest of their stay in the school, and up until they wrote their final examinations, their attitude towards me changed completely. They became friendly and spoke to me with a kind of respect I had not noticed before.

That experience encouraged me to do even better in my academics. I strived harder — though the "outing" habits remained.

Fourth Form completed, most of my classmates were made various prefects — Head Boy, Vice Head Boy, House Captains, Vice House Captains, Labor Prefect, Social Prefect, Food Prefect, and others.

On vacation day, we all left school for our various destinations. I left for Sabon Gari, Zaria.

FIFTH FORM

Returning to school in September as a Fifth Former felt different. School years during my primary education used to run from January to December. When I was admitted into secondary school, the school year also started in January. However, in the middle of my Second Form, the school calendar changed. Year Two was completed in June instead of December. The summer holidays were from the end of June to the end of August. Form Three commenced in September of the same year and was completed within that new cycle.

Having gone through so much as a junior student, I was now a senior — a Fifth Former!

On my arrival at our dormitory, Crowther House, I was welcomed by our House Captain, who had some gossip to share. He had just learned from a reliable source that a seventh dormitory, Aminu House, would be opened to students. The new dormitory would be populated by students selected from different classes and from the other six houses — Kalejaiye, Crowther, Johnston, Jones, Smith, and Mort — and that I would be named the first House Captain of the new house. The choice, he said, was made by the principal based on academic performance.

I was apprehensive. I had never seen myself as someone to be considered for such a position. I had never lobbied, begged, or bent my principles to gain any advantage or position of authority. I was just myself.

His source turned out to be very accurate. At the first assembly of the year, I was named the first House Captain of the seventh dormitory — Aminu House of St. Paul's College, Wusasa, Zaria (now Kufena College, Wusasa, Zaria). This change took place when the school calendar was adjusted and the schools were taken over by the state governments.

We had a break from school, and I was home on vacation as a prefect — the House Captain of the newest house in Kufena College, Wusasa, Zaria. Christmas was good, and by January we were back in school.

In February, we woke up in school to the news that a dastardly act had been committed by some renegade members of the Nigerian Army against their Commander-in-Chief and members of his staff on his way to work that fateful Friday morning. He had no motorcade or retinue of bodyguards. His life was cut short in the streets of Ikoyi, Lagos.

The news brought a sense of doom and gloom over the entire school. Classes were called off for the day. Some of us seized the opportunity to go to Sabon Gari to while away the time and see how the general public was reacting beyond the school fence. The general who was gunned down had been a well-liked Head of State, and sadness filled the town. People wept openly.

We huddled together in a bar, discussing the situation and our upcoming West African School Certificate mock examinations. We reminisced about how things used to be when the school was still St. Paul's College — before it was taken over by the state government and renamed Kufena College.

We talked about how prefects were now being disrespected by junior students who ran to the principal with every complaint. The principal had warned against the excessive display of seniority and the handling of junior students, and he often ruled in favor of the complainants — even going as far as ordering corporal punishment for some prefects.

There was also talk that some prefects were considering relinquishing their positions and, in a dramatic gesture, handing back their caps — the symbol of a prefect's authority — publicly during school assembly.

Other concerns were raised about the quality of school meals and the attitude of the school sergeant, whose sole duty was to flog erring students at the order of the school authorities, the principal, or his vice.

While we sat drinking and snacking on cow-foot pepper soup, conversation about the coup attempt and the assassination continued, with each new report bringing more details of the unfolding event.

We all left to catch a bus back to Wusasa before dinner time. The day was treated as an "Outing Saturday."

Little did I know that most of the issues casually raised earlier — concerning the principal's attitude toward complaints from junior students, and the frustrations of disgruntled prefects — would come up again in discussions among different groups.

Attempts by some of us to push the school to reconsider its stance on exercising seniority over junior students, and other related matters, would later shape the lives of some of us involved.

We had put the assassination of the Head of State behind us. The military handled the situation in their usual way, and the country moved on.

The Fifth Formers of Kufena College were now preparing to write their mock examinations ahead of the June West African School Certificate Examination. Most of us were already dreaming of undergraduate admission later that year.

After completing the mock exams, the Fifth Formers anxiously waited for the various subject teachers to finish marking and scoring the scripts. It took forever.

The delay in releasing the mock exam results — results that were often used for gaining provisional admission into tertiary institutions pending the release of the actual WAEC results — caused a great deal of anxiety and tension in the school.

The attitude of the school authorities, especially the vice principal, who regularly employed the school sergeant to flog students regardless of their status — prefect or not — infuriated many Fifth Formers. Most looked back on the three or more years they had endured "discipline" from seniors with regret and disappointment. They had now become seniors themselves, yet they were not allowed to exercise any seniority.

Things reached a boiling point when some prefects, led by a house captain, decided to relinquish their authority and publicly dropped their caps — the symbol of their office — before the principal.

The situation grew tense, and rumors began flying around.

I got an earful of complaints. People found me easy to approach — empathetic and a good listener. I received invitations from various groups to join their discussions, and I usually honored them. The complaints all centered around the same themes.

One such gathering was an expanded group that included some members of our "Outing Saturday" circle and others who were deeply concerned about the non-release of the mock examination results.

Meetings were now held in the middle of the football field in the evenings after games. I presided over the meetings; I was the only prefect — a house captain — in this group of about twelve students. I had access to the principal and could hold my own in any conversation with him. This must have informed the decision of different Fifth Formers to reach out to me with their concerns.

What would all these meetings lead to? We resolved to take action.

Could the decision to hold clandestine meetings and plan what later resembled a coup plot have come from our analyzing past military events? Anyway, we went ahead with an elaborate plan to organize a "Como" — we simply remembered the "Como" from our first week in Form One. The elaborate planning to draw the attention of the authorities involved instigating and actually creating a commotion, a "Como," leading to a breakdown of law and order in the school, akin to the first Como. This would be more serious. This was our Plan B.

Plan A involved only myself requesting a meeting on behalf of the aggrieved Fifth Formers to air their grievances — because I was a school prefect, a house captain, and was known to be favored by the principal. After all, he had chosen me, on academic grounds, to be the first House Captain of the new Aminu House.

Fate always has a hand in men's affairs. A member of our group came to one of our meetings with his weed-smoking pal. This did not go down well with the rest of the group. He vouched for his pal, and we allowed them into the meeting — our undoing, a monumental mistake.

Probably in one of the hallucination-induced spells of this fellow's pal, the tag-along headed straight to spill our plans. He stuck to spilling Plan B — the commotion part of our scheme.

He failed to inform the principal of the group's Plan A — the honest discussion I intended to have with the principal on behalf of the students to find ways to resolve the issues without recourse to violence. His mind did not work that way. To his weed-befuddled brain, the plan to foment a "Como" seemed the best thing to spill.

He mentioned names, including mine, as the leader of the group. He went into step-by-step details of Plan B.

One evening, I had just woken from my afternoon nap, preparing for an all-nighter with my reading pal — my best friend and a member of Aminu House who shares the same first name as our house. Still groggy from sleep and the day's activities, the head boy, who shares the same room with me, came in with a serious look and told me the principal wanted to see me. That was unusual; the principal was never known to work this late.

The head boy noticed the perplexed look on my face and said rumors had reached him that some student had gone all the way to the principal's house — the principal lived quite a distance from school — and had told him everything. Now the principal was summoning me.

On my way to the principal's office that late evening, I stopped in the study classroom to drop my books and materials. Arriving at the principal's door, I knocked politely and was invited in by his stern voice. There was no offer of a seat; I wasn't expecting one. He went straight to the point and asked me to tell him everything I knew about the impending "Como."

I explained Plan A — that I intended to request a meeting with him to outline the several gatherings and the complaints from the Fifth Formers and prefects. I also told him about the concerns regarding the vice-principal and his habit of using the school sergeant to whip erring senior students, whether they were prefects or not.

Not surprisingly, the principal listened attentively to my presentation, taking notes as I spoke. When I was done, he simply asked what our next course of action would be now that he was aware of our group's grievances.

That night, before taking my leave from the principal's office, I pleaded for a couple of days to gather the group and ask that we all stand down on any planned action. The principal promised to look into all the issues raised and come up with a solution that would guarantee peace in the school.

I gave him my word that there would be no disruptions or "Como" of any sort to normal school activities. He believed me — I knew because he told me so.

I was about to experience my second major disappointment, shock, and surprise in life. Fate plays an integral part in every human journey; I believe that completely.

I felt relieved after my conversation with the principal that night. I was confident that once I called a meeting, the group would stand down since Plan A was already in motion. The principal had promised to address all grievances and concerns.

But the very next night, an incident occurred between the school's dining hall and Smith House. Rumors had already spread that a group was planning a "Como" and had been exposed by a snitch who reported everything to the principal.

The noise around the school was that I had been invited to the principal's office to explain all I knew about the planned "Como." The name of the snitch was also being mentioned in the rumors making the rounds.

Unfortunately, the night after my visit to the principal's office, the "snitch" was walking from Mort House toward Smith House, just around the dining hall, when he saw another student approaching from the opposite direction holding a makeshift field hockey stick, popularly called a *Gora*.

As both made eye contact, the entire school compound experienced a brief power outage. The "snitch" panicked and took off running straight out of the school compound to the principal's house, several kilometers away.

What a coincidence! The group's plan had involved switching off the school's power supply to trigger the commotion. The "snitch," seeing the student from Smith House holding the *Gora* and heading his way, thought the plan had begun and that he was being targeted for betraying us.

The student with the stick at that time was not aware of any plans; he wasn't even a member of the group. He held the stick for a totally different reason and was walking in the direction he was heading for that reason alone. Coincidence and fate dragged him and members of our group into a big trouble — trouble he did not ask for or foresee.

The principal kept the snitch in his house overnight for protection. He later drove to the school, and the power outage was restored; the disruption lasted only a few minutes. Students went about their normal activities and nobody knew that a report had been made to the principal. I was not aware of any of this. It was said that the principal stayed late into the night before heading home for some rest.

The next day another rumor spread: a disciplinary committee from the Ministry of Education in Kaduna would come to interrogate and decide the fate of the planners of the "Como." The story included the snitch's claim that his life had been threatened because of the incident with the innocent student and his *Gora.*

After morning assembly, the principal was not available to conduct it as he usually did; he was busy in his office. We had all settled in our classrooms when each member of our group was summoned to the principal's office, escorted by the school sergeant. Unknown to us, a detachment of anti-riot police officers was already stationed outside the school premises near the railway tracks, waiting for orders.

Each student summoned to the principal's office faced a panel of civil servants from the Kaduna State Education Board. Questions were asked to establish identity, and then each student was asked to say what they knew about the planned "Como."

I was the last to face the interrogation panel. When I got into the principal's office, he looked me straight in the face and said he was disappointed in me, that he believed in me, and that I betrayed his trust. I gave my word to him, and I failed because a student's life was threatened. Without flinching, I looked straight into his eyes and said that if he believed he made a wrong decision by appointing me a house captain and believing in me, then that is on him. But I know that I did not betray him; he did not allow me to put in motion the peace process we agreed upon, and he was hasty in coming to a conclusion concerning the events of the previous night.

After we were interrogated individually, we were asked to wait outside the principal's office. The disciplinary committee was left to deliberate and decide our fate.

At this time, the detachment of law enforcement had been summoned, their vehicle parked close to the principal's office. This was ominous. Most of the members of the group just interrogated were not even aware of the events of the last two nights. They were neither aware of my late summons two nights ago to the principal's office nor were they aware of the snitch racing to report a false alarm story to the principal in his home.

This group was perplexed, worried, and scared as they awaited the decision of the committee. There was apprehension and tension in the air. The whole school was eerily quiet.

After the committee concluded its deliberations, we were summoned all at once into the principal's office, standing side by side facing the panel with our backs to the longest wall in the space but not resting on the wall.

After a long and convoluted address by the chairman of the panel to justify the verdict of guilty on all of us and the punishment of indefinite suspension from school pending ratification by the Kaduna State Commissioner for Education.

A palpable silence could be felt in the room. Some of the "accused" fell into some sort of shock; some had sheepish smiles on their faces. I felt anger well up inside me. I knew an injustice had just been done to us. We would not be allowed to write the West African School Certificate Exams in June. Our lives had just been put on hold, even slated for destruction, so it felt.

We were escorted by a fully armed police officer to retrieve our property from our dormitories, then returned to the classroom area where the school van — as we called the Bedford 5-ton truck — was parked, its back built with wood and rows of wooden benches bolted to provide seats for passengers.

This "van" was used for conveying students to all outside activities, such as conveying the sick to Tudun Wada General Hospital, Muslims to the Zaria City Central Mosque for Friday Jumaat prayers, and football and other sports teams and their supporters to "away" games.

We were herded into this van, popularly called "gongworo," because of its wobbly and uncomfortable nature in and out of the slightest road bumps and puddles.

With our luggage hurriedly packed, still dumbfounded and confused, we remained silent. Usually, the trip would have ended at the motor park located at Wusasa Market, but it was as if the driver had been instructed to take us as far away from the school as possible. The driver dropped us off at the Sabon Gari Motor Park, directly behind St. George's Anglican Church — my family church, where I was baptized as a baby, where mummy was known and well respected —

a place almost like a second home during breaks from school.

Sometimes I wonder if mummy was carefully pointing out, by some of her actions when I was growing up, that the journey of life is full of surprises and that life might spring one or more surprises at any time in the journey.

I remember that mummy would always inform us of the name and place and how long she intended to stay if she went visiting any family friends, such as her adopted mama Saro, sick church or market colleagues, newborn babies and their families, and other numerous social or community volunteer visits.

Two days after the July 1966 attack and killings of a certain ethnic group of Nigerians in Zaria, as "retaliation" for the events of the January 1966 violent military coup, mummy had not seen or heard from a number of colleagues and family friends. She was anxious for them, and she decided to pay them a visit.

I still do not know why she had me in tow. I was quite young, and before then had never seen a corpse in my entire life. While we sidestepped dead humans in various states of decomposition, I avoided looking directly at any one corpse and just covered my nose to the stench.

I wondered why human beings would do this kind of horrendous damage to themselves. Maybe mummy wanted me to see the extent human beings can go to justify anything. She probably was preparing me to understand that life's journey may sometimes be shocking, gory, and unpredictable.

The realization that I would not be writing the WAEC examinations in June hit me hard. My feelings alighting from the school's "gongworo" were of shock and disbelief that human beings are capable of manipulating any situation to achieve predetermined outcomes. The verdict of indefinite suspension stank of manipulation and pre-determination.

Just like the eventful swimming incident of years back, this event—the indefinite suspension of fourteen fifth formers of Kufena College, Wusasa, Zaria—spread into Sabon Gari like wild harmattan fire. The Sabon Gari market was buzzing; sympathizers converged around mummy's stalls to express their shock and outrage at such a decision by the school and to glean the latest gossipy information filtering slowly into the marketplace.

Meanwhile, after we all got down from "gongworo," perplexed, we decided to visit the nearest bar to gather our thoughts and plan next steps.

Some members of our group lived in Kaduna and some in Kano, a couple of us in Sabon Gari, Zaria.

We were drinking alcohol, and one or two members also engaged the coin slot machine. After getting enough drinks to induce "Dutch courage," we decided to go home to our parents, determined to explain the situation as best as we could and face the consequences. We said our bye-byes; the Sabon Gari folks waited until the others boarded transport to their various destinations. That was the last time some of us ever set eyes on each other again—ever!

Mummy has this cold, piercing, almost dead look in her eyes when she is grieving. I had seen this look when any member of our church or someone she knew died.

One hot afternoon, while trekking home from school, I observed a group of people in front of my friend and classmate's house. I thought nothing of it. There was a poster of an obituary, but I did not stop to read it.

Mummy was at home—very unusual. That was when I noticed the cold, piercing, dead look in her eyes. She told me that my friend and classmate's mother had died earlier that morning after a brief illness. She was only twenty-six years old.

That was the same face and look that confronted me when I arrived home. My acquired "Dutch courage" dissolved the moment I met her piercing, accusing eyes asking *why?* —all without uttering a single word. I felt the pain piercing her heart.

A few months earlier, she was invited to our school's end-of-year awards ceremony. She had a front-row seat and was one of the proud parents whose son had achieved academic excellence in his final class. I was first in my class in the promotion examinations from fourth form to fifth and final form.

The newly turbaned Emir of Zaria (Zazzau) was on hand to present certificates of excellence to recipients. I was among them.

Mummy was so excited and proud of me. The photo of me shaking hands with the Emir was her trophy for all her struggles to see her children succeed. I was on the road to success. She enlarged and displayed this photo in her living room. Then this happened!

SELF-EXILE TO KANO

The stigma of knowing that one's name had been splashed across at least two prominent national newspapers as the leader of a group of students planning to cause confusion and instigate a riot to disrupt school activities was beginning to weigh down on mummy. Her silence became eerie as she went around wearing that dead look on her face.

I confined myself to a room in the old vicarage of our church. My friend and I shared the room—our hideout during breaks from school.

The only bright spot in these dark times was that classmates, former school seniors, and well-wishers sent registration forms for the upcoming November–December General Certificate of Education (GCE), urging me to apply for the examinations.

Mummy and I were now having a conversation on the way forward for the first time since I arrived from school, expelled.

She still would not ask what exactly transpired or led to the "indefinite suspension." Instead, she requested that I take the advice of one of my aunties to repeat fifth form in a school in faraway Bendel State. I had never travelled that far from Zaria, let alone for school, and I declined the offer.

Politely, I informed mummy that I had never failed or repeated a class. She reminded me that it was very difficult to pass the GCE exams, which were considered tougher than the WAEC exams, and besides, I would be writing them from home, away from any school setting.

Mummy resigned herself to allowing me to complete the forms for the November–December GCE examinations. She provided the application fee on one condition: I had to go on "exile" and leave Zaria.

I completed one of the numerous forms sent to me by well-wishers and selected an examination center in Kano. Kano was the obvious choice for my exile. Our eldest sister, now married with kids, resided in Kano—so did my immediate elder sister.

Arrangements were made for me to stay with my immediate elder sister and her husband; they had no children at that time.

I gathered my possessions—books and study materials—and headed for the Nigerian Railway Station to catch the train arriving from Lagos and heading to the northern city of Kano.

Sitting and trying to finish a novel by James Hadley Chase, which I had been attempting to complete since my forced vacation from school, I found my mind all over the place. I could not concentrate. Even on this journey from Zaria to Kaduna, I still could not focus. Normally, it would take me half a day to read any novel by the same author from cover to cover.

Finally, we arrived at the Kano Railway Station. I alighted, collected my luggage from the overhead bin, and found my way to my sister's home.

The events leading to and culminating in my being out of school all took place in April. The WAEC exams for my classmates were to commence in May–June.

Here I was in Kano in the month of May, instead of reading for those exams, fueling the bad habits—especially drinking—that I had cultivated in about five years of boarding school life.

The thought of the November–December GCE examinations was now buried deep at the back of my mind. I shut out everything concerning school or exams and sought solace in all the wrong places.

My sister made it her duty to send news back to mummy about my bad habits—bar crawling and chasing after ladies—another acquired taste, honed by our "outing Saturday" escapades from school.

Mummy would hop on the next train to Kano to plead with me to cut down on my drinking and other vices. I simply told her that I knew what I was doing and that, at the right time, everything would fall into place. I was not sure she believed me, but I am sure she hoped.

Mummy never liked to sleep in any bed other than her own; she would never dream of spending the night at her in-laws'.

After pleading with me and advising caution in my lifestyle, she would then present me with goodies such as fried beef and other snacks. She never failed to bring me some pocket money too.

By evening, mummy would be ready to start her return trip home to Zaria. I usually escorted her to the train station, and on the way, she would express optimism about my health and cheerful spirits. She believed I would succeed in my effort to write the November–December GCE exams, which many considered nearly impossible to pass due to the high failure rate and the disadvantage of writing outside a formal school environment.

My best friend and reading buddy from school made it a point of duty to visit mummy at her market stall on his "outing Saturdays." Mummy always told me about his visits whenever she came to Kano to check up on me. He never failed to assure her of his confidence in my academic ability and his belief that I would do well in the November–December GCE exams, regardless of others' doubts about their difficulty. He was truly my friend.

Meanwhile, by mid-May, my classmates had begun writing their May–June WAEC exams. I was aware—it made me sad—and I buried myself further in drinking and bar crawling.

One of my classmates, who had written the exams, came visiting afterward. He lived in Kano and was employed in the grocery department of a multinational corporation's Kano branch, working in the meat section. I visited him at work during his lunch hour. He provided me relief from spending too much time alone. I now had a companion and a buddy in Kano.

One afternoon, after my buddy was done with work, he visited to break the good news that the results of the May–June exams were out. He did very well and reeled out the results of as many of our classmates as he could remember. My reading buddy and best friend—the one who visited mummy at her market stall to encourage her on my account—passed with flying colors and was the best student in almost all the subjects he took. I was highly impressed but not surprised. He was a genius.

This news—of my classmates' results and their performances—became my wake-up call. In my heart, I immediately resolved to start studying in earnest for my upcoming GCE examinations starting in early November. I had a couple of weeks in September and the whole of October to get my act together.

Three of my former seniors from school lived in Kano. They had fallen short in their WAEC examinations taken the previous May–June, before my classmates sat for theirs. They were now registered to take the November–December examinations, same as me.

These former seniors visited to request that I join them in preparation for the exams and form a study group, with me taking the lead in Chemistry and Biology. I agreed. We met in my room every day, and I studied on my own at night. Some days, I visited the Kano Central Library for a change of scene and to enjoy the ambience of a library.

My sister, who had always reported my lack of seriousness to mummy—prompting her frequent visits to Kano—was now concerned that I was studying too hard. I was constantly pulling all-nighters. This turn of events in my attitude toward studies was also conveyed to mummy. The report, however, was not considered harmful enough to warrant a visit. Mummy let me be on this one.

There was one local man, a Hausa farmer, who often saw me sitting outside watching people and vehicles pass by whenever I wasn't studying. We always exchanged greetings on his way to and from his farm.

When I became serious with my preparation, I was rarely outside. One day, I stepped out for a change of scene, and he was excited to see me. He asked where I had been, and I told him about my upcoming examinations and studying. He asked if I pulled all-nighters, and I replied in the affirmative.

He promised me that on his way back from the farm the next day, he would bring me a root, and that I should make myself available. He kept his promise. The next day, he brought me a small piece of root. I was to take only a tiny bite of it and chew it with a bite of kola nut. Kola nuts are known to contain some caffeine. I neither knew the name of the root nor its composition.

When I was about to begin studying for the night, I took a tiny bite of the root and another bite of kola nut, chewing both thoroughly and swallowing the mixture. Studying was progressing in earnest. As the night grew older, it seemed the overhead electric bulb I used became brighter. I noticed I was neither yawning nor feeling any fatigue or tiredness. I kept covering material after material. Night became day, and I was still studying.

By mid-morning, my three study friends arrived. I was still at my desk, feeling fresh and going on as if all was well. I couldn't keep this good feeling to myself, so I told them about the mysterious root–kola nut combination and offered them a little piece to try. All three declined my offer.

At the usual time, after study practice, the three members of our group took their leave, and I was alone again. I continued studying. After forty-eight hours awake, I began to feel uneasy and concerned for myself.

My sister had also noticed that I had not been sleeping nor eating well. She did not ask, and I did not tell her anything about my mysterious root and kola nut business.

By now, I was worried enough to visit the chemist shop. A chemist shop, like a "bodega," was a place where both off-the-counter and "prescription" medicines could be purchased. The owners would also administer first aid and sometimes even prescribe medication and give injections to willing clients.

I was forced to visit because I hadn't slept in over forty-eight hours as a result of chewing that small combination of root and kola nut to stay awake. After listening to my symptoms, the attendant prescribed and sold me some bluish sleeping pills. As soon as I arrived back in my room, I swallowed the pills with some water. About an hour later, I was passed out in a very deep sleep.

My sister, who offered me accommodation, became very worried as I slept for a whole day. I did not wake up for any meals. This situation was soon reported to mummy in Zaria.

Your guess is as good as mine—that was my last experience chewing that root–kola-nut combination.

I complained to the farmer, and he told me that I must have chewed more than the little he prescribed. Anyway, I never used the remaining root or any other medicine or concoction to stay awake through the remaining days of preparation for my examinations.

My reading friends and I were rounding off our studies, preparing for the examinations. We practiced past questions in the different subjects we had registered for and held verbal question-and-answer sessions on topics common to the group. The study group was helpful. It strengthened the confidence I had in myself that I would pass the examination with enough credits to qualify for admission into an undergraduate course in any university.

Suddenly, the much-awaited month of November arrived. Examination "fever" was in the air—last-minute revisions, questions and answers, cross-checking notes, and labeling diagrams in biology, physics, chemistry, and geography. Mathematical problems and formulae were revised and practiced; English did not pose much of a problem in its preparation.

All six subjects I registered for, I wrote. There were many words of admonition from concerned friends who got wind that I had registered for only six subjects. They were all of the opinion that I had not given myself any room for error. Usually, final-year students registered for and sat for a minimum of eight subjects in the WAEC or the GCE.

Obtaining strong credits in at least five subjects with the right combinations guaranteed admission and a place in the university to pursue an undergraduate degree.

Most people felt that registering and sitting for only six subjects was cutting it too thin. But that was the level of confidence I had in my ability. With the benefit of hindsight, I now know that a supreme being is in control of all the outcomes of my life experiences. I could not explain my confidence that I would pass my GCE exams, obtain the required credits, and be admitted into undergraduate studies.

After writing the exams, the waiting period—from the end of November to sometime in April, when results were expected—was a downtime of doing nothing. It was very easy to fall back into old habits, bar crawling and drinking.

Sometimes, my in-laws, especially our eldest sister's husband, would take me along to some of the parties he was invited to. His friends knew me; they also knew I could put away a few bottles quickly. They were never quite sure of my status—I was neither working nor in school. They simply assumed I was just a loafer.

One evening in April of the following year, after I had written my November–December GCE examinations, my immediate elder sister's husband—the one I had been living with since my self-exile from Zaria—walked up to inform me that the evening news on television had announced the release of the last GCE results, and that I should go check mine.

I could hardly breathe after hearing this. It was already late, and I felt it was too late to go to the West African

Examinations Council offices to find out about my results. I decided to wait until the next day.

That night, sleep eluded me, even after consuming a good amount of alcohol. My thoughts were filled with apprehension and confusion—the "what ifs" and all the arguments people had made that I had risked everything by sitting for only six subjects came rushing through my mind. I became scared, worried, and unsure of myself throughout the night. For the first time, I second-guessed myself and almost doubted my own capability—and the Supreme Being who had always been in my corner.

At daybreak, still groggy from the effects of the previous night's alcohol and restless from lack of sleep, I summoned courage and completed my morning hygiene routine. I boarded public transport to the WAEC offices. From the gates to the information boards, where printed copies of the results were posted according to surnames in alphabetical order, it was bedlam—a sea of heads, people walking to and fro, some towards the boards, others away.

Almost all those coming away from the boards wore gloomy faces. Some wailed openly; others lamented their fate quietly. Those of us heading towards the boards did so with trepidation, anticipation, and a touch of optimism.

When I arrived at the WAEC premises, I suddenly felt confident, optimistic, and hopeful. Reaching the board where my name was posted, it was not difficult to find it— someone had underlined it boldly with a pencil, along with all six subjects and their respective grades.

On that sheet, and in that entire section of the board, my name stood out because of the bold underline. I had passed all six subjects and earned very good credits—enough to qualify for admission into any science-related faculty as an undergraduate student.

I could not hide my excitement. I shouted aloud, "That is me!" As I was writing down my results on a piece of paper, questions followed my announcement: "Is it true?" "Are you really the owner of this amazing result?" "How did you manage it?" "You must be very brilliant!" the crowd said, one after another. The people around me went on and on.

After carefully writing down my results, I began walking towards the gate. It felt as though I was walking on air. People pointed, nodded, and some just stared at me.

I was so excited I could hardly remember the bus ride home. There were no cell phones at that time, so I had to wait until the next day for my in-law to call mummy in Zaria by leaving a message with one of our neighbors who worked for the Post and Telecommunications department (P&T).

When I finally arrived home, my sister and her husband were having lunch. Before they could ask me any questions, I simply handed them the sheet of paper with my results. I was overwhelmed with emotion and could not utter a word. The look of surprise and astonishment on their faces spoke volumes.

When they finally found their voices, the gist of what I heard was, "We know you are brilliant—but GCE? How did you manage it with all your bar crawling and all?" I just smiled, politely excused myself, and told them I wanted to go inform our eldest sister and her husband.

I knew that our eldest sister and her husband only needed a good excuse to throw an impromptu party—and there was no better reason than this. Once I showed them my results, a gathering of their friends was called. Drinks and food flowed freely.

It was at this gathering, after a good number of drinks, that the conversation turned to disbelief—how they never knew I was even studying, let alone writing exams, and now here I was with such grades and talks of university education. To them, it sounded like a fairy tale. Alcohol and laughter flowed till late into the night.

The next day, and in the days that followed, I could feel the respect and admiration of everyone around me. I was grateful for that. I kept imagining how mummy would feel hearing this good news.

Mummy sent congratulatory messages but did not want me to return to Zaria at that time. She prayed instead for a triumphant entry into Zaria later—to make up for the shame of my self-exile.

A neighbor of our eldest sister, who had attended the impromptu celebration party that night and now saw me in a different light, promised to find me a job pending my admission into the university. She kept her promise.

GHOST WORKERS

The job I was introduced to involved construction site payroll for one of the largest housing project companies operating in Kano at that time. The construction site had a Welsh man as Project Manager and a young thirty-three-year-old Nigerian billionaire as the Chairman and Chief Executive of the company.

At every visit to the site, the Chairman always expressed dissatisfaction with the pace of the project and would take out his frustration on the Welshman, threatening to send him packing back to Wales with immediate effect. I always considered their spats both funny and a form of grandstanding by the company Chairman.

This job was my first ever. I was quite young, naïve, and full of brilliant ideas. I needed to start saving for my anticipated admission into the university.

It was from this job that I learned another of life's lessons—my third—that in life, what you see might not be what you get. My first experience had been missing out on admission into St. Paul's College after Primary Six, having to complete Primary Seven despite my brilliance. The second was the series of events that conspired to push me out before completing Fifth Form and writing the West African School Certificate Examination (WAEC), forcing me into exile from my beloved Sabon Gari Zaria to Kano to write the General Certificate of Education (GCE).

Now, I was about to have my third life lesson—this one not adversely affecting me, but serving as an eye-opener to the ways and dealings of adults in our environment, especially in financial matters.

This housing project was one of the largest in the whole of Northern Nigeria at that time. Construction was divided into zones. Arriving in Kano from Zaria, sprawling new buildings confronted the eye—a clear sign of growth and foresight by the then government of Kano State.

The zoning of the estate was according to bedroom types: there were two-, three-, and four-bedroom bungalows under construction.

Construction administration was done according to zones, and so also were hiring and payroll administration. Each zone had its own foreman, with an overall site foreman appointed to supervise them all. Tradesmen—masons, carpenters, laborers, electricians, and others—were sought after every day.

Zonal foremen hired laborers in their droves. They simply asked each new hire for two passport photographs, affixed one to an employment card, and had the worker either sign or thumbprint it for identification. The site foreman approved all new hires by delegating the recruitment process to the zonal foremen. Zonal foremen were very powerful, as I later found out.

Our office was located in the main site building, where we had the offices of the Site Project Manager, Site Financial Manager, and Site Accountant. The general open office, equipped with desks and chairs, was occupied by a crew of site payroll clerks—I was one of them. I was a payroll clerk. It was my first ever job, and it happened to be in the largest housing project in the city of Kano, Northern Nigeria. I was proud of the job, even though I saw it as temporary, pending my admission into the university.

The Site Accountant was our direct supervisor. We reported to him. My duty, like that of the other payroll clerks, was to enter the names of employees in the zones allocated to us. Each zone had workers from all trades, including laborers.

The employment cards, each affixed with a passport photograph and either a signature or thumbprint, were sent to us by the zonal foremen upon hire. We then entered the information into the payroll sheets, after which the employment cards were stored.

There were neither computers nor electronic spreadsheets for this job. Every piece of information was entered manually onto printed sheets, and figures were computed later using electronic calculators and adding machines.

A day before payday, all payroll clerks would have computed the total amount of cash required to be paid out to workers in their respective zones, based on the figures submitted by the site foremen. The information included individual hours worked and rate of pay. On the payroll sheet, apart from the employee's full name, were listed the trade, rate of pay, and hours worked.

After computing the total sum to be paid out, a breakdown into currency denominations was also required.

These figures were submitted to the Financial Manager for transmission to the bank a day before payday.

On payday, a convoy of cars—the Site Financial Manager, the Site Accountant in their respective vehicles, and the payroll clerks with wooden boxes in pickup vans—set out for the bank, surrounded by gun-toting police security.

Each of us clerks were assigned a bank clerk responsible for filling our orders according to the breakdown of currency denominations submitted the previous day. Once this was completed, the convoy headed back to the project site offices.

Each clerk would then count out the various denominations and insert the total amount into envelopes with pre-written names from the payroll sheets. When the process of filling the pay envelopes was completed for each zone, the next step was for the zonal foremen to stop work in their zones and lead a procession of their workers to the window where we, the payroll clerks, waited with smiles plastered on our faces, ready to dole out envelopes.

We shouted out names; faces appeared at our windows. We verified identities by checking the affixed photo on the employment card, then asked for a signature or thumbprint as indicated on the card. We went through all the names on our payroll sheets, repeating the names of unclaimed envelopes.

The next day, we waited for anyone who had missed out the previous day—one more day of grace—and all "unclaimed wages," still in their envelopes, were submitted to the Site Accountant.

The Site Accountant was supposed to return these unclaimed monies to the company's bank account. I often worked extra hours to help reconcile the unclaimed wages, removing money from the envelopes, tallying the total, and submitting a reconciliation report to the Site Accountant.

The first time I worked overtime for him, he volunteered to give me a ride into town because, at that hour, there was no public transport available—the construction site was located on the outskirts of Kano.

I was also given a sum of money—fifty Naira. That was a lot of money to me at that time; in fact, it was good money. I was grateful for the largesse, and the amount formed the base of my "back to school" funds.

I never thought much about the reconciliation of unclaimed wages, my working overtime, or the gift from the Site Accountant—until certain events began to unfold around the construction site.

At lunch hour the day after payday, I had not brought lunch to work as I often did. It was my way of saving my meagre funds. So, I accompanied one of my colleagues, also a payroll clerk, to one of the building site locations. There was a local food shack—a *buka*—where food was prepared and sold. Most of the site supervisors and workers converged there at lunchtime for their meals.

I liked the variety and choices of food available, so I ordered a meal that I could afford according to my wages.

To my surprise, two of my colleagues looked at my meal order, snickered derisively, and asked if that was all I was going to eat. I replied that it was what I could afford.

When their own orders arrived, the meat portions were separate from the main meal—their plates were loaded with all sorts of meat, fish, and chicken. I wondered how on earth they could afford such meals. They invited me to join them and share, but I declined politely.

On my way back to the office after lunch, I could not stop wondering how those two colleagues of mine—and the site foremen—were able to afford the kind of meals I had just seen.

I did not have to wonder for long. I began to notice some frenetic activities, hush-hush conversations, and the exchange of documents between site foremen and a few of my colleagues, the payroll clerks. One colleague of mine, with whom I sometimes conversed and exchanged reading materials, was approached by a desperate site foreman who asked him to try and co-opt me into their scheme.

What was this scheme of theirs? The site foremen would scout neighboring hamlets and villages to locate willing locals, just to acquire their passport photographs. They paid to have the photos taken. These photos later appeared on bogus employment cards, which were either thumb-printed or signed.

These fake employments were then presented to colluding payroll clerks, who entered the information from the cards into the payroll sheets. At the end of the month, the site foremen submitted time sheets for their so-called "ghost workers."

On payday, either the actual people whose photos appeared on the employment cards would show up to collect their wages—after signing or thumb-printing to confirm payment—or the conniving payroll clerk would extract the bogus pay envelopes on the instruction of their conspiring site foreman.

Where an actual person signed and collected a pay envelope for a job they never did, the proceeds inside the envelope were shared between the site foreman and the individual according to a prearranged formula.

In other cases, where there were no actual people to sign for the envelopes, the site foreman himself would sign or thumb-print on the wage sheet for as many envelopes as were retrieved by the payroll clerk. The contents of these envelopes were then shared as previously agreed.

Interestingly, some of the people who agreed to come and collect the envelopes never showed up on payday, not even forty-eight hours after. Any "ghost" envelopes not extracted before the end of the day were still accounted for, and the site accountant became aware of the so-called unclaimed wages by close of business on payday. Except for a few genuine cases, nobody ever showed up for those wages. These were the envelopes the site accountant always instructed me to reconcile and hand over to him. I later realized he never returned these amounts to the company's account.

My third life lesson introduced me to how adults might behave in their quest for financial acquisition, gain, and appropriation—or, as it were, misappropriation. The shock was that while I was striving at my job as a payroll clerk, ensuring that all tasks assigned to me were done to near perfection and on time, others were perfecting ways to steal. I was always the first to complete my assigned zone's monthly payroll, including the tabulation and breakdown of currency denominations as required by the banks for disbursement. While I toiled, a group of people had constituted themselves into a clique, siphoning money illegally from the same company that employed them and ensured their wages were paid as and when due.

Shocking was my discovery that the unclaimed wages from the nefarious activities of that clique of thieving employees ended up in the pocket of the Site Accountant. He was never one to question the number of unclaimed pay envelopes every month. The Financial Manager had no clue what was going on. The Site Accountant ensured that only the unclaimed wages of actual registered employees were submitted for accounting.

He always cross-checked with the employment cards. He was adept at knowing which cards were bogus. He had his methods. No wonder the Site Accountant was always trying to convince me to set aside my plans for a university education, promising that working with him would be worthwhile for me in the long run. He would say that if I continued working with him, I could make a lot of money for myself.

I always replied by repeating what mummy had told me since I was little: that for whatever it was worth, I must ensure I obtained at least an undergraduate degree—what is known as a first degree. Mummy always said that one may obtain a first degree in any field of study, after which one could decide what direction to pursue in education and career.

I knew there was no way I would ignore the wise sayings of mummy for some undefined future. Besides, money did not have much hold on my life at that early age, and even now at a much older age.

The last I heard of that group—the first set of colleagues I ever had in my first job—was that their gig was exposed. Some of them were arrested; some fled the country before the law caught up with them. The Site Accountant was accused of negligence and lack of foresight by the Chairman of the company. He walked away with a slap on the wrist— he was from the same village, the ancestral home of the Chairman.

That was another lesson in how some adults conduct their business.

MY CHILDHOOD FRIEND

There were these very exciting years between my swimming adventure and gaining admission into St. Paul's College, Wusasa, Zaria. I met a friend who became my very close friend. We were inseparable. He was one year and two weeks older than me. We met when I was eight and he was nine.

His father had just been consecrated the Archdeacon of the Diocese of Zaria, Anglican Communion, and posted from his duty as Deacon of St. Bartholomew's Church, Wusasa, Zaria, to our own St. George's Anglican Church, Sabon Gari, Zaria.

My young friend was riding his bicycle around the church, which was very close to the main market. I was just exiting the market when we saw each other. The connection was instantaneous. We hit it off right away, started chatting, and became friends. He invited me to the vicarage, their home. After a lot of questioning by his mother—who instantly became *mama* to me, as she was to all of them— she welcomed me warmly.

Mama discovered from our conversation that long before I was born, they had been neighbors with my parents in Kaduna—news to me. I was excited, and so was my new friend. Mama asked me to tell mummy when I got home that she sent her greetings.

A strong bond of friendship was rekindled between mummy and mama, between my friend and me—a bond that went beyond friendship and crossed into the realm of family. We became family, with very deep ties.

My friend and I played every day from breakfast to dinner. It got to a point where I stayed so long in his home that I began spending the nights with his family. We were that close. We ate from the same plate and slept in the same room.

My friend was very talented. He rode his bicycle from Sabon Gari to Wusasa to deliver hot loaves of bread to the kitchen at St. Luke's Hospital, Wusasa. He was good at making "catapult" slings and using them to take down stationary or flying birds, especially doves. He reared pigeons.

He could swim—I was not allowed to swim, you remember? He could knit too. We had a wooden knitting equipment with a rectangular gap in the middle, nails on both sides of the gap, and an extra nail on either side. With this, we knitted neck scarves called "mufflers." We created various colorful designs.

My friend was also adept at sports—high jump, javelin, and sprint. He played ping-pong, "table tennis." His presence around any barbershop that displayed a ping-pong table guaranteed the business a lot of customers. My friend was a ping-pong champion; he defeated all comers at the barbershop, ensuring quick turn-overs and revenue for the owner.

After breakfast on Saturdays, mama always required our services to place her freshly baked loaves of bread into plastic bags and add paper labels. This was a job my friend and I enjoyed. We had free access to oven-fresh bread and margarine. After completing the bagging, mama sometimes asked us to count the money she had collected from sales. When we finished counting, she rewarded each of us with some money.

One of our relaxation spots was the Nigerian Railway Station. We would visit, take our seats on the long wooden benches fixed to the floor of the platform, and simply while away time.

Such visits were almost always after mama's largesse. The money she gave us, we used to buy boiled guinea fowl eggs. This was where my friend's talent came into play: we ate a lot of eggs without spending much money. One of his gifts was the ability to determine the strength of a boiled guinea fowl egg's shell just by tapping its tip with his fingernail.

Playing and "chopping" guinea fowl eggs was a pastime akin to gambling. You bought eggs from a guinea fowl egg hawker by first testing the strength of the shell. Then you went into a bet with another buyer. One of you placed your egg between your thumb and index finger, holding it tight. The other buyer slammed the tip of their egg against the tip of the egg being held. Whichever egg cracked was "chopped" by the owner of the egg that remained intact.

My friend sometimes chopped a dozen eggs. He even set a record of a dozen and a half chopped eggs in one sitting.

We simply sat on the wooden bench at the railway station and devoured the "chopped" eggs.

We also liked to stay close to home, especially when we were knitting a "muffler." We would sit on a pile of cement blocks earmarked for the new church building, a project that had been in the pipeline for years.

Those rows and layers of cement blocks, lined along the vicarage fence by the garage, provided us a vintage sitting position. My friend and I would sit on the low fence by the driveway, with the collection of cement blocks beside us. In the yard for the proposed new church building were plum trees bearing red succulent cherry-like fruits.

We sat on the low fence and the cement blocks arranged about fifty–six layers high. We sucked on the plum fruits we had plucked earlier while we knitted our mufflers, chatting away and generally having a good time. Sometimes we were carried away by the different things happening on the street across from us. We would drop our knitting pins into the deep holes in the cement blocks—irretrievable. We lost many pins to those holes.

We each bought ourselves a leather belt—nice pieces. We did not only use the belts to hold up our pants; we sometimes employed them as weapons of provocation and attack.

Whenever we became bored, we would prowl some streets close to home, looking for boys our age. If we found any, we used our belts to take a few swipes at the unfortunate victim, after which we ran home.

One eventful day, we encountered two boys our age. We went on the attack with our belts. But these boys did not cower like the others; they gave us a good fight—a real run for our money. We fled home, this time not in the exhilaration and fun of accomplishment, but in a flight of self-preservation. On this day, we bit more than we could chew.

Our fun times came to a halt when my friend went off to boarding school in faraway Kwatarkwashi, in the then North Western State of Nigeria. He was one year and two weeks older than me. He gained admission after completing Primary Six from St. Bartholomew's Primary School in Wusasa. I did not change schools when the family moved from Wusasa to Sabon Gari.

After my friend's departure, I felt empty and had a lot of time on my hands. I was completing my Class Seven in primary school, preparing for my First School Leaving Certificate Examinations (FSLC) and the Common Entrance Examination for admission into secondary education.

During the first term vacation from his new school, I noticed a new way of talking and behaving in my friend. It was interesting because it showed how quickly boarding house education could reshape a boy's perspective.

My friend became chattier—I had always thought *I* was the talkative one. His demonstrations as he described events and places around his new school were very animated. He was livelier.

The reason for this chatty and animated behavior was that he was now doing much better in his academics. He understood more of what he was being taught and was genuinely learning in school. He was now posting better marks in his class tests. He was very happy that he could contribute more in class discussions. This newfound academic revival worked magic on him, and he continued to improve. He later in life became a professor.

JOINING A UNIVERSITY

Gaining admission into the university, I later came to know, did not begin and end with obtaining a good result in WAEC or GCE. There were other factors—a young boy like me was just learning. Life is not what it seems. There is always more beneath the surface.

The brilliant and well-connected classmates of mine in St. Paul's College, Wusasa, Zaria, who wrote the June–July WAEC exams and earned good grades in their later-released mock WAEC results (the non-release of our mock WAEC exams was one of the reasons for planning the "Como") were offered provisional admissions into Basic Schools and other institutions of higher learning.

Basic Schools were affiliated with some universities, especially in Northern Nigeria at that time. They were preparatory institutions for gaining admission into university faculties. Brilliant students would spend one year in Basic Schools and obtain qualifications comparable to completing a two-year Higher School Certificate (HSC) program.

So, while my classmates—those who were not expelled and had the prerequisites—were offered provisional admission in August and were already close to completing their Basic School education, I was still waiting to get into Basic School after them. That, to me, was close enough.

Obtaining admission now proved a herculean task, despite the fact that I already had the necessary academic requirements. My form had been placed in a closet with other applications marked **NOT QUALIFIED**.

After the long wait for a call-up letter into the Basic School, our hope was based solely on the strength of my GCE performance, and nothing else. It now appeared that mummy and I were waiting in vain.

Mummy decided to seek the help of her friend, mama. Mama was requested to discuss the matter with the Archdeacon—her husband—whom we also called papa. Mama informed papa that I already had my GCE results with all the requisite credits and, by the university's requirement, was qualified for admission into the Basic School's Interim Joint Matriculation Board (IJMB) program.

At this time, students had already resumed classes. I was still at home, hoping and waiting. Papa finally agreed to visit the Principal of the School of Basic Studies.

Papa, just like the principal, was flabbergasted that my application file was not in the regular bin for consideration. After a thorough search ordered by the principal, the clerks in his office located my file in a storage pile classified as *Not Qualified for Admission*. The principal was stunned when he looked through my file and my GCE results. He immediately offered me admission into the School of Basic Studies. By then, I had missed more than a month of lectures and learning.

Papa was proud that he had been able to accomplish something noble. He helped revive my dreams. He was instrumental in rescuing my file, which had been hidden under a pile of "rejects."

As if resuming a month and a half into a nine-month course was not challenging enough—the School of Basic Studies being a compressed, fast-track interim schooling preparatory for university admission—the HSC program normally ran for eighteen months. Now I had lost one and a half months from a nine-month compressed course.

And as if this was not problem enough, a few months into my studies, while I was still catching up with copying notes and trying to make up for all the classes I had missed while awaiting admission, something happened nationwide—an event that caused a mammoth disruption in my studies.

The National Union of Nigerian Students (NUNS), as it was then known, announced a nationwide protest against the arbitrary increase in feeding fees for meals in cafeterias across all Federal University campuses. These protests, more often than not, degenerated into chaos. This one, christened *Ali-must-go*, was no different.

Anarchy and chaos descended on our campus. The detachment of Nigerian soldiers stationed at the Nigerian Army Depot, Sabon Gari, Zaria, was invited to quell the riots that erupted from what was initially tagged a "peaceful protest."

After three days of bedlam, which resulted in a few lost lives, the university authorities announced the closure of both campuses in Samaru and Kongo.

By the time students were allowed to resume, and the hiked cafeteria fees still stood, it was already time for students to write the end-of-year examinations—Basic School students included.

Preparation for the IJMB examinations was tough as it were, even tougher for me, who had arrived one and a half months late due to my delayed admission, and now had missed additional time because of the riots, campus closure, and suspension of academic activities.

Study sessions were disorganized. A lot of material had never been covered in lectures. There were not enough lecture notes. The university library was not available at the time of the school closure. Preparation for the IJMB examinations was indeed grueling.

The final examination timetable was published. Examinations were written. Later, results were also released.

Next came waiting. Waiting for the Joint Admissions and Matriculation Board (JAMB) to publish the names of candidates, their chosen faculties, and the universities offering admission.

I waited patiently. Factors such as the state where one's parents originated from, and the grades in the examination, were major determinants for offers into first, second, and third choices of universities and faculties.

I make no excuses, but I must state that six months of preparation for an examination in a course normally completed in eighteen months—and the "state of origin" of my parents (even though I had neither been to those parts nor ever lived there)—did not favor me in gaining admission into any of my chosen faculties. Still, I waited patiently.

I remember clearly one Sunday morning, while my friends and I were lolling in bed "gisting," when I heard a loud "Congratulations!" shouted in my direction. The person shouting looked up from the Sunday newspaper he had been engrossed in. My name was in the advertised pages of the latest list of faculty admissions published by JAMB. I was offered admission into the Faculty of Science with a major in Chemistry.

After confirming by looking at the publication myself, I rushed out to get a copy of the Sunday newspaper. Then I rushed off to Sabon Gari, to mummy. I broke the news to her and showed her the publication. I still remember the proud look in her eyes and her smile.

I thought mummy might be disappointed that I did not get into any of the faculties of my choice. As if reading my thoughts, she reiterated what she had been telling me since I was younger: *Get an undergraduate degree in any field of study; after that, you will determine what you want to do.*

She asked if I would be comfortable as a Chemistry major, and I proudly said yes. That settled it for her.

My first year in the Faculty of Science was like that of many university students—more partying than studying. The year ended without protests or riots. No lockouts.

I started Year Two in September, and in October, after thirteen years of military intervention, the country ushered in a civilian government. The new civilian president was sworn in on the first day of October. I remember that day because mummy had keenly followed all the presidential parties, their campaigns, and their promises.

Mummy was pleased that she would once again witness a civilian administration. The inauguration and swearing-in ceremony of the new president was televised live. Mummy was glued to the television, watching every step of the ceremony. This remains one of those events I vividly remember mummy showing genuine interest in—almost becoming part of it through the television screen.

After a carefree first year, I promised myself that I would want to end my undergraduate degree as a first-class student. Like the promises I make to myself, I intended to keep it.

Some Biology and Chemistry courses for Year Three students in the Faculty of Education were combined with Year Two students in the Faculty of Science. Once Year Two commenced, my goal was to achieve an "A" grade in all tests and examinations.

The very first test grades I received were straight A(s), keeping the promise I made to myself. After the first of October inauguration of the new civilian president, it became difficult for me to pin mummy down. I wanted to show her my test papers, to let her know my promise of graduating in the first class, and that I had started to accumulate the grades necessary to achieve my goal. Strange, anytime I travelled from Samaru to Sabon-Gari to visit mummy, I met her absence. Even though absent, mummy would always leave a bowl of fried beef or guinea fowl or some combination of beef and guinea fowl. This, she placed in a covered bowl at the same spot as when I was in the secondary school at Wusasa.

This was going on week-in week-out, my visit and her absence. I found it rather strange. Mummy was either visiting a sick person, a family that just had a newborn, some family mourning, or some others preparing for marriage. She was always on the move on these social and philanthropic visits. But she already knew the days and times of my visits. Could she not make time to at least see me briefly? Even though she unfailingly left me a treat, always.

On one of my visits around the third week of November, I bought a Christmas card intended for mummy. After all, December was approaching, and cost-wise, that was a better time for preparations. On this visit, like in previous visits, she was not at home. I became frustrated. I felt something was not right, but I couldn't place my finger on the "something."

NYSC

A couple of weeks later, that *something* manifested itself. That *something* became the most catastrophic event of my life. It changed the trajectory of my life, affected my being, and changed me forever. That singular event dashed my hopes, questioned my trust in God, "blurred" my vision, killed my drive and ambition. It left me hanging.

One of my close friends from secondary school attended the famed Barewa College situated in the district of Gaskiya in Zaria. Barewa College was tagged the school that produced Heads of State and Presidents. We became friends when we were introduced by his uncle, who was then serving as a Curate in St. George's Anglican Church.

My friend lived in Lagos, the big city. He would normally arrive in Zaria about a week before school resumed after each term's vacation. We had about a week to play around before he went back to school. Our friendship continued in the School of Basic Studies.

In my short few months of playing catch-up in the School of Basic Studies due to my late admission, I cultivated the habit of taking notes in my own rough "shorthand." When studying, I rewrote these notes in a neat "longhand"—clear and legible. These legible notes served two purposes: they helped me remember salient points as I rewrote them, and they made for easier study during tests and examination periods.

When the university campus was shut down due to the *Ali-must-go* riots, my friend and his sister had to head back to Lagos. They normally travelled by air—Nigerian Airways from Kaduna to Lagos. But the urgency of the shutdown, and the panic following news of students killed during the military intervention, left little time to procure airline tickets.

My friend and his sister were placed on a bus from Kaduna to Lagos. They travelled by road. The bus arrived in Lagos in the early hours of the following day.

As they alighted from the bus, they waited to walk across the pedestrian flyover to the opposite side of the bus stop and trek home. Their home was less than half an hour's walk from the bus stop.

They were about to step onto the overhead bridge when a vehicle, speeding at a frightening pace, suddenly screeched to a halt and parked right under the bridge. Gun-toting men jumped out, rushed toward my friend and his sister, and dispossessed them of every single piece of luggage and their purses. They were left with nothing—but thankfully, they were unharmed.

Shaken and scared, they hurriedly crossed to the other side, holding hands and running across the eight-lane highway, avoiding the pedestrian crossing. They arrived home panting, frightened, and still very much shaken.

Their parents were terrified as well, but thankful that the children were unhurt. They vowed never again to allow them to take a public bus for any trip to or from school, no matter the situation. They stuck strictly to air travel throughout their university days.

As they began recovering from the robbery and the long bus ride, my friend and his sister became worried about their study materials—all of which had been in their stolen luggage. My friend told his father that he had a reliable source in Zaria from whom he could obtain reading materials.

A return ticket was purchased for him. He landed at Kaduna Airport, where a driver from one of the numerous companies his father chaired—or served as a board member—was waiting to receive him. The driver had clear instructions to take him to Zaria and bring him back to the airport when he was done.

My friend suddenly appeared before me in the room at the "old vicarage," where we all hung out during vacations. I was surprised to see him. He narrated his and his sister's ordeal at the hands of the gun-toting robbers, and the loss of all their possessions, including their study materials.

He said he had told his father that I was the only trusted resource who could help them out of their situation. I felt proud that my friend could recommend me so highly to his father. I gave him all my neat notes in all subjects—we were all enrolled in the same classes. I decided to rely on my rough notes written in my "short hand." I also provided him with my textbooks.

My friend was so happy that I did not disappoint him. He was proud of my kind and selfless gesture. I was proud of myself too.

This act of selflessness did not go unnoticed. When the campus closure was lifted and students resumed, my friend's father accompanied him and his sister back to campus. He came to see me and personally thanked me. He promised that if I ever needed any help—now or after graduation—I should not hesitate to ask him. I was elated. By a simple act of kindness, I had gained a very powerful connection.

Whenever I found myself in Lagos during vacations, I always visited their home. I was always well received.

One or two years later—I cannot remember exactly what we were doing on this fateful day—my friend was called away to receive news from home. His father had been involved in a road accident and was hospitalized in Jos.

My friend's father usually travelled by air whenever he was on one of his numerous business trips. But on this particular trip, he and one of his business partners were traveling by road from Kaduna to Jos, a distance of 216 km, about a four-hour journey.

The car they were travelling in blew a tire somewhere close to Jos. After a few somersaults, it landed back on its "feet." My friend's father, his business partner, and their driver were all rushed to a hospital in Jos. My friend's father managed to speak with his family, and they were relieved to hear that everyone involved had been stabilized and was doing well—or so they thought.

The next day, while we were relaxing in our room—my friend was one of my roommates, three of us classmates shared a room—he was called away again for an update on his father. But this time, the news was ominous and devastating. His father had passed on, due to complications from undetected internal bleeding.

My first direct connection to a powerful and wealthy Nigerian dissolved into the night.

My friend and his sister were inconsolable. It was difficult to watch them go through so much grief. It was heart-wrenching.

After a while, like everything in life, my friend and his sister moved on, continued with their education, and adjusted as best they could. I visited their home in Lagos anytime I found myself in the city. You could feel the emptiness in that home—the vacuum left by a powerful, yet very kind and loving father. The death of my friend's father took a massive toll on him and completely changed the trajectory of his life.

Upon completion of an undergraduate degree, all new graduates are enlisted into a Federal Government National Youth Service program—the NYSC. This service is a corps program intended to integrate the society by allowing young adults to live and work among communities in different geopolitical zones from their own.

New graduates from Northern Nigeria are typically posted to states in Southern Nigeria, and vice versa.

An initial camping period, about one month, is conducted at designated camp locations in state capitals, often within the campus of a higher institution of learning.

I was posted to a state in the South-Eastern part of Nigeria. I was born and bred in Northern Nigeria. Until then, I had never been to any part of Eastern Nigeria. I had only heard news about the area—usually in connection with comments about the Nigerian civil war.

So, my posting to Eastern Nigeria was a welcome development for me. I was excited—excited that I could finally see firsthand the places I had only read about as theatres of the civil war.

I was on my way to my posting just as the civilian government of the day had won a landslide second-term election victory. Civilians were still at the helm of government at all levels.

Arriving in the capital of the state where I was posted for my NYSC camp and subsequent primary assignment was exciting. I loved the greenery, the neat roads, and the proper drainage.

NYSC camp was located in a College of Education, a higher institution of learning. At the time of the civil war, the Eastern States were referred to as the heartland of Eastern Nigeria.

We were allocated dormitories—double and single bunk beds—khaki uniforms in military style, boots, NYSC-emblazoned face caps, and other necessary camp clothing.

Every NYSC member is assigned to a squadron. Each squadron leader is responsible for ensuring that squad members get up as soon as the bugle is sounded very early in the morning. Each squadron then heads for the main sports field, lined up by squadrons, with each squadron leader at the front.

The camp commander arrives and proceeds to issue commands, military-style. Camp commanders are military officers. Drills are led by non-commissioned military officers, while squadron leaders ensure that commands are passed down to all members of their squad. There is always a daily roll call.

I never liked the military drills, especially marching in formation. I always feigned injury. This pretend injury granted me exemption from marching. Those of us who feigned injury were called "Lazy Coppers." Later in the evening, some of us would go out to play football (soccer).

After a month in the NYSC camp—filled with military-style drills, games, lectures on various human-angle topics, humanitarian work, and volunteer activities—came the passing out from camp and the posting to primary assignments.

Postings to primary assignments, like everything in Nigeria at that time, involved lobbying for "juicy" or "favorable" placements. Just as candidates lobbied for favorable NYSC state postings, they also lobbied for favorable primary assignments—usually in more cosmopolitan states or places with potential employment opportunities after the one-year service.

I refused to influence my posting. I accepted my posting to this Eastern State. I also did not heed the prompting and prodding of colleagues to go into town and lobby for postings in industries or corporate organizations. I simply accepted my posting to teach in a village in the hinterland of the state.

On the day of resumption for our primary postings, I gathered all my possessions from the camp dormitory and proceeded to the information board. I located my name and my posting—it was a secondary school in some remote part of the state.

I hung around the waiting area, knowing that school principals often came to pick up their allotted "coppers," as NYSC members were fondly called. My principal soon arrived, looking for me and any other copper posted to his school. He held a placard with the name of his school. I walked up to him and introduced myself. He was so excited to find a young man ready to accompany him straightaway to his school and become one of his youth corps members.

Following his instructions, I loaded my suitcase into his vehicle, sat in the front passenger seat with him driving, and we headed out of town into the hinterland. He inundated me with stories of how, in years past—including the most recent year—the coppers allocated to his school would promise that they wanted to take a day or two off before coming. They never showed up. He was surprised and pleased that I was willing to follow him immediately.

On our way, he deliberately took a route that passed over a wooden bridge constructed during the civil war by the

Nigerian Army Engineering Corps, led by a brigadier general who later became a military head of state. My host also pointed out buildings still bearing bullet holes from the civil war that had ended some eleven years earlier.

On arrival at the school premises, the principal—my host—drove straight to his residence. There, I was warmly welcomed by his amiable and motherly wife. She was also a teacher in the school. She, too, expressed surprise that I had come along immediately. She had a meal already prepared for all of us. I enjoyed a well-prepared meal. The principal offered drinks, and I accepted a beer.

I was then taken to the coppers' quarters—the residence for male members of the NYSC. I was the first male copper to arrive, so I had first pick of the living space.

The principal instructed me to come to his residence three times a day for my meals until such a time as I was equipped to start cooking my own. I enjoyed the hospitality of this exceptionally accommodating family for one whole week. The matriarch's cooking was excellent at all times.

After we had lunch and a beer on my first day, my host decided to introduce me to the village. He took me to a nice place for drinks and game meat—referred to as "bush meat," mostly greater cane rat ("grasscutter") or antelope. That day, the choice was peppered grasscutter, which we washed down with bottles of beer. I was full and declined their invitation to dinner later that night.

The routine of my meals with my hosts continued for one week. At each meal, I received an invitation; one of their younger children was always sent to come and call me over. This happened unfailingly at every mealtime.

After one week, I now had my pots, pans, cutlery, and stove. At this point, I remembered mummy—she would have made sure these supplies accompanied me either to camp, or she would have insisted I visit her before reporting for my primary assignment. Now I was equipped and ready to prepare my own meals. I informed my host and thanked the family for their uncommon hospitality and their acceptance of my person.

Two weeks after I settled in, my roommate showed up. He had driven into the school premises with his cousin a week earlier. He was upset that he did not get a "good" posting. He had lobbied unsuccessfully for any posting other than teaching in what he called a "village school."

When he came in to speak rudely to the school principal and began berating the school, I had no choice but to intervene. I told him that I had accepted to stay so I could serve—NYSC is for service, not a luxury expedition. I explained that I was gradually settling in, and if he agreed to settle down, we could make our experience in the "village school" interesting and worthwhile.

A week after my pep talk—two weeks after his tantrums—my roommate finally agreed to settle into life in the "village school." Shortly after, two female NYSC members also arrived for their primary postings. They settled into the female quarters.

Just when we thought we were only four NYSC members in the school, a few weeks later, another female

NYSC member joined us. Her father had been promised that after NYSC camp in the state she was posted to, she would be relocated to her home state to serve her primary assignment in the school where he was the principal and her mother a teacher.

The new female corps member was the last child and only daughter of the principal of the school where I was serving my primary posting—my host, whose family had shown me such great hospitality. She was also a science teacher. Things got interesting.

WATERSIDE CONFESSIONS

One day, my "quarters mate"—now my friend, down from his high horse and truly enjoying our little environment—and I were invited out by a prince of the village. He took us out in his fancy car for drinks and bush meat. We did not arrive back at our accommodation until very late that night.

My friend who lost his father years earlier in that road accident along the Kaduna–Jos highway had been waiting for my arrival. He had come from the capital of a neighboring state. Things had not been good for him. Ever since he lost his dad in that unfortunate accident, his life had taken a downward spiral.

He was unable to secure a faculty admission after Basic School, so he transferred to another Federal university located in a central northern state. After his third year, he was rusticated. He then enrolled in the Nigerian Naval School to complete the Naval Officers Course. During the final examinations, the authorities found an excuse to remove him from the course—thereby terminating what could have been his saving grace.

He was in the middle of this crisis, with nowhere to go, when he remembered someone had informed him that I was in this village for my NYSC. He packed up, boarded public transportation, and arrived at my place of primary assignment.

A very big hug followed. When I asked whether he had eaten since arriving and not finding me, he informed me that once the principal and his family found out my "brother" came visiting, he was offered food and drinks. He had been taken care of—thanks to the hospitality of my principal and his caring family.

Sometimes in life, there are certain unplanned occurrences that appear destined. One such occurrence was when the science teachers in the school held a meeting to prepare the final-year students for their science practical examinations.

I was the school's senior Chemistry teacher; the principal's daughter was the senior Biology teacher—both of us members of the NYSC. The senior Physics teacher was a permanent staff member of the school.

At the meeting of the school's senior science teachers, it was resolved that materials for that year's Biology practical would be better obtained in the capital city of the neighboring state.

I knew that city fairly well. My NYSC male colleague was from that part of the state. We visited at least once a month to squander, in one night, our entire stipends—always in the same nightclub.

After squandering our stipend, we arrived back at our quarters dead broke. One month is a long time—an especially long time when waiting for another stipend. My colleague was adept at securing what he wanted on credit. He would walk into shops run by some women and open a credit account: a note detailing all provisions collected within the month. Credit was due and payable on the next payday.

He had the same kind of account in the cafeteria located in the NYSC secretariat. This was where our monthly stipend was disbursed. He would normally eat a large meal and drink bottles of beer on credit. Once he collected his stipend, he paid the cafeteria woman. On his way home to the village, he stopped over to pay the women in the shops where his credit was open.

Whatever balance was left of the stipend, he contributed to our transportation and night clubbing in the city. We visited his home in the wee hours of the morning after leaving the nightclub. We always went to the same club. It was, at that time, the "talk of the town."

So, when the idea of purchasing materials for the science practicals from this same city was mentioned at the science teachers' meeting, I felt we were in familiar territory. At least I could find my way to my friend's home in that city. I had been introduced to his family—particularly his brothers.

Little did I know that our biology teacher had all *her* plans nailed down. She was not going to follow her family to their country home for the weekend. She planned to use the time to prepare for the forthcoming Biology WAEC practical examinations for her fifth-form students. That science teachers' meeting was to impress her father, the principal, and also provide cover for her real intentions.

I had an eye for her, but the hospitality of her family made such thoughts—anything beyond professional conversation—a no-go area. She had other plans.

On the day she planned her travels to purchase the biology materials, she stopped over at our quarters and casually invited me to journey with her. I was totally taken unawares. I did not even have enough time to think about her request or inform my friends.

I still had enough presence of mind to ask if her parents knew she was travelling, and whether she would be coming back the same day. She casually told me that she was alone for the weekend—her family had travelled to their country home for a getaway.

I was curiously elated; excitement almost burst out of my chest. She then told me we were not making a straight journey. She knew of a fancy restaurant in a neighboring city. We should first make that trip, have lunch there, and then proceed to our final destination.

We did exactly as she planned—ate a nice meal in the fancy restaurant. By this time, we both could not hold back our intentions. We were holding hands, smiling, and just enjoying our moment.

On arrival at our final destination, we headed straight to the waterside market. Fish and all kinds of sea animals were sold there. We scouted for the required sea crustaceans needed for that year's WAEC Biology practicals and purchased the necessary preservatives to keep them "fresh" until required.

On our way, in the public transportation, I subtly informed my female colleague that our male colleague had a home in the city and that we could seek accommodation for the night if we ran late and were unable to travel back to our duty post after our purchases. She agreed, and a plan was put in place: eat dinner and retire early.

We arrived at my male colleague's home in the city with our purchases. I introduced my female colleague to the group as our biology teacher and fellow NYSC member. We were warmly received, even though I had given them no prior notice, and their brother—my colleague—was unaware of my whereabouts, talk less of my being in his ancestral home.

We were invited to dinner. We accepted, and all of us went to a restaurant. My colleague's brothers invited his girlfriend, who lived in the same vicinity as them. She asked after her boyfriend, and I responded that he was doing well, but I did not mention that he had no idea where I was.

After dinner, we all went back to their large compound. There were various single-room apartments with outdoor conveniences. Bathrooms were built and fenced with corrugated iron sheets. If you needed to go out at night, you carried a torchlight or a kerosene lamp— "lantern."

We were shown a room—it doubled as a living room and a bedroom. One of my friend's brothers relinquished his apartment for us. My friend's girlfriend offered to accommodate my female colleague for the night, but she politely declined.

This group of nice people were very accommodating. They even offered to take us nightclubbing, but my colleague begged off—she had a slight headache, a very convenient excuse. We were then left alone. We were now by ourselves in a city, sharing the same bed that had been relinquished to accommodate us for the night.

We chatted for a long time, got to know each other better, and actually confessed to harboring some feelings for each other. That night, we developed a strong bond of friendship that lasted throughout our NYSC service year.

The next morning, we prepared for our return journey amidst curious looks and unspoken questions. We thanked our hosts and simply left them with no answers—as no questions were asked.

On arrival home, my female colleague's family had still not returned from their weekend getaway. We had enough time to explore some places in town and appreciate one another.

We kept our newfound friendship to ourselves. We behaved as professional colleagues in the presence of others, especially within the school environment.

My male colleague and roommate did not suspect any new behavior, and I did not tell him about our trip or our visit to his home. His brothers and girlfriend narrated everything to him when he visited home.

He was mad at me for keeping such a secret from him. He watched both of us closely, but we never gave him any reason to suspect anything, and the stories told to him by his family about our visit almost sounded like a fairy tale. I eventually confessed that we were indeed in his home and were well taken care of by his brothers and his girlfriend. He was shocked by our audacious outing.

My friendship with my female colleague was one of mutual respect. We kept it very close. Somehow, I knew her mother sensed that there was something between her daughter and me. She also seemed to suspect when I had not eaten a good meal in a while. She would prepare a sumptuous meal and send it to me.

I normally shared these meals with my male colleague and my friend who now resided with me. We were all in a fix as to what next steps he should take. The Naval School had expelled him.

My obligation to my friend was to ensure he never brought harm to himself on account of all the negative things happening in his life. Coming to live with me at the lowest point of his life—and my providing a roof over his head, comfort to his soul, keeping him alive, and helping him believe and hope again—is one of my life's achievements. I am grateful to God Almighty for granting me the opportunity to be available, to be used to provide hope and succor to a fellow human being and a friend.

My friendship with my female NYSC colleague was a highlight of my service year. We took trips to Kaduna and to Lagos during our service year. Her elder brother lived and worked in Kaduna, and one of her uncles lived and worked in Lagos.

When we planned such trips—if her trip was for a week—I would request permission to be away for two weeks. I would request permission for a trip to Lagos when our intended destination was Kaduna, and vice versa. The first week, I stayed with other NYSC colleagues at another location. My principal only knew that I was out of town.

On the appointed morning of her trip, I would purchase a bus ticket, then stay hidden some distance away from the bus. Her father brought her to the bus terminal. As soon as she boarded the bus and he drove off, I would come out of my hiding place and board the same bus. She always had a seat reserved for me. We then enjoyed our trip to our predetermined destination.

Upon arrival, we disembarked at separate stops. I always got off earlier, at a different bus stop in town, and spent a day or two with other NYSC colleagues. Meanwhile, she arrived at the main bus terminal to journey home with her father, who awaited her arrival.

I will never know if anyone ever noticed that both of us were always away around the same time and arrived back almost at the same time. These travels continued throughout our NYSC service year.

When the service year was over, she travelled to visit me—either in Lagos or Kaduna—wherever I happened to be at the time.

As the service year drew to a close, the thought of *what next* loomed large in my mind. Obtaining gainful employment was first and foremost in my thoughts. Graduate unemployment had reached an all-time high; having appropriate connections was almost necessary to securing any worthwhile job.

For this reason, I decided to take an exploratory trip to Zaria, retrace my roots, and reconnect with some influential people. It was on this trip that I learned my childhood friend—the same friend with whom I knitted mufflers and ate countless guinea fowl eggs at the railway station—was planning his wedding.

I stayed in Zaria for two weeks with my friend. We met with other childhood friends every evening for drinks, and we also hatched plans for his wedding.

The father of one of the friends we hung out with was very helpful. He promised to introduce me to an executive in the Federal Government Corporation responsible for oil and gas exploration and distribution. He even endorsed the back of his complimentary card for me to take along as confirmation that I had his personal backing.

I kept the card safe. It remained with me at all times throughout my period of job searching.

We concluded planning and arrangements for my friend's bachelor party and wedding after-party. My two-week holiday was over. I returned to my base to complete my service year.

The service year ended with the passing-out parade and the receipt of the NYSC certificate.

I had a heart-to-heart discussion with my friend who had been expelled from the Naval College and had spent the entire service year with me. I pleaded with him to return home, explain his situation, and prepare to chart a new course for his life. He took my advice, and we both journeyed back to Lagos. We did not see each other again until many years later.

While we were in the university, this same friend—who was later rusticated from the Naval Academy—had been a member of the University Drama Society. The society was a collection of male and female students from different backgrounds and faculties. Students of English Literature, Drama, International Studies, and even Chemistry were members.

Sometime in my first year, he asked me to accompany him to one of the Drama Society's rehearsals. The society staged plays across different campuses, and the gate fees collected were used to sustain the group's needs: purchase of props, food, and other materials required to put on a good show. I was encouraged by the professional way the group conducted its activities. I made up my mind to be part of this group.

By the time I was in Year Two, I had become an integral member of the society. I began appearing in lead roles in some of our staged plays.

I was able to successfully combine my growing interest in stage acting with my academic responsibilities and covered a lot of ground in Year Two.

After so many attempts to reach mummy—my weekly visits home and her repeated absence, despite the treats she always left for me—I decided to focus on my schoolwork and the stage plays.

We had just performed an amazing play for our main-campus audience and were preparing to take the play on the road to Congo Campus and later to other institutions of higher learning in and around Zaria.

I was resting in my room. Until this day, no member of my family had ever visited me on campus. It had never been necessary because I was always visiting them on weekends.

This weekday, I was called out by a neighbor who told me I had a visitor—one of my sisters, the middle one of my three sisters. She was the closest to mummy; they ran both her stalls in the market together, and in addition, she taught school.

The moment she laid her eyes on me, she started weeping uncontrollably, yelling and bawling. When we were finally able to calm her down, she announced that mummy was ill and on admission in the hospital—the general hospital in Tudun-Wada.

This was news to me. All my life, mummy had never been taken ill to the point of hospitalization, nor had she ever been so sick that she could not speak. That was the condition my sister described.

I left everything I was engaged in and immediately followed her to the hospital. On arrival, we were allowed to visit mummy at her bedside. Mummy could neither open her eyes nor speak. She was just murmuring incoherently.

Mummy's younger sister, our aunt, murmured into her ear, telling her that I was around. Then mummy began to call my native name—on and on.

My aunt told me that I had met mummy in an improved condition, that she had been far worse when she was brought in. I told her that if this weakened state was the "improved condition," then mummy must have arrived in a terrible state indeed.

My aunt was an experienced nurse in the same hospital. She made it known that she had summoned all the clout she had to ensure mummy received the best care from the hospital staff, especially from the doctors and nurses.

After leaving the hospital—deeply disappointed in mummy's condition, even with all the stops my aunt had pulled—I did not feel comfortable, especially as the lab results had not been able to definitively diagnose what was wrong with her.

I was all along in the bus to school reliving my doubts and misgivings. Why did mummy have tears rolling down her closed eyes? Why was she constantly calling my name?

How I was able to gather my thoughts and pull out one of my best performances that night was nothing short of a miracle. The audience gave a standing ovation to our performance that evening—the same evening my mummy was lying in a hospital bed, diagnosis unknown.

After our performance, during the debriefing session, I told the group about my personal situation and mummy's condition. The group individually expressed their support and offered their prayers.

The next day we had no show—our day off. I spent the entire day sleeping and recovering from the emotional weight of the news and the previous day's exertions. I was exhausted emotionally.

In my mind, I thought that if I took the next day off from all activities, including visiting mummy, then perhaps by the following day, if I went to see her, by some miracle she would be in a much-improved condition.

Was I expecting the lab results to finally arrive and assist the doctors in making a proper diagnosis? And thereafter, would they administer the appropriate medicines, and she would suddenly be better than the previous day? Was I simply too scared of the condition I might find mummy in if I visited again? I had no answers.

On this day, we were to take our play on the road to Congo Campus. I was scheduled to be part of the performance, hoping to deliver something close to the previous day's performance.

My plan was to wash my costume, air-dry it, and iron it later in the day before the evening show. After doing my laundry, I intended to visit mummy—after all, I had let a day pass without visiting her, hoping I would find a better, stronger mummy.

As I was doing laundry in front of my hostel, suddenly a visitor appeared. It was my friend's sister—our big sister— the eldest of our church Archdeacon's children, a very sweet lady. She always treated me with respect, my young age notwithstanding. I guessed she respected my studious disposition and intellect.

I should have been suspicious of her sudden presence at my accommodation, but I was too excited to see her. She asked if I had been to see mummy in the hospital. I told her I was just planning to finish my laundry and head there. She said I shouldn't worry; she had just arrived from Kaduna and had received the news that mummy was in the hospital. She planned to visit her and offered me a ride. I accepted.

I noticed a slight diversion from the route that would lead to Tudun-Wada—the location of the general hospital. She explained that she wanted to pick up a basket of provisions for mummy from home in Sabon Gari. At this point, I still wasn't suspicious. I wasn't thinking anything uncomfortable.

But as soon as she drove into the street where home was—the vicarage—I saw a number of our church members gathered in clusters along the street, talking in whispers.

A HEART STILL HANGING

It suddenly dawned on me. I had witnessed so many of such ominous gatherings. It happened when a member of our congregation was announced dead.

Mummy is gone. Exactly—gone.

I rushed out of the car. No one said a word to me; they did not need to. I rushed past mama—she was wailing in the sitting room. She had just lost a very dear friend. The church had lost an outstanding member. The community had lost one of their best.

I had just lost the meaning of life.

Darkness clouded me. In the haze of my mind, I heard a nurse suggest that I be sedated. I ignored everyone and their suggestions and headed straight to our room in the old vicarage. I just sat on my bed, staring into space.

This is the *catastrophic something* I mentioned earlier—the most catastrophic event of my life. The event that changed the trajectory of my life, affected my very being, and altered me forever.

This singular event—the sudden and unexpected death of mummy—dashed my hopes, questioned my trust in God, "blurred" my vision, killed my drive and ambition. Left me hanging. I did not recover from the shock and the aftermath of mummy's passing unto glory. Well over four decades now, and counting. The pain is still fresh and acute.

Needless to say, the whole play and activities of our drama society were suspended by the executive of the club. That same evening, they all gathered in the university's luxury bus to pay me and our family a condolence visit. It was very touching. I am forever grateful and appreciative of the respect and love shown to me at the lowest point of my life.

Mummy left this sinful world on the last day of November. She lived for only fifty-one years.

After her burial a few days later, I went back to the university in a haze. I was practically a shell of myself. Hollow.

I had lost interest in any and everything.

I told myself over and over again that the only reason I always strived to be the best in all I did, and to always better myself, was because I had only ever been in competition with one person—myself. That competition ceased abruptly. There was no more reason to be better at anything.

The woman who gave her all died before she could share in the great milestones I had been dreaming of. She sold wares in her shop during the day, passed the time preparing sponge from scratch for sale, taught after-school classes, and sewed clothes late into the night—with tears in her eyes and pain in her heart—unsure of how she would cope providing for her four surviving children.

Now that I was in my second year of undergraduate studies, pulling "A" grades in tests and examinations, ready to conquer the world with great ideas forming in my head… now that I was becoming popular acting in stage plays and drawing crowds… things were just beginning to fall into place.

I had dreamed of how mummy would be well taken care of, how she would live in my home, how she would help take care of my children—her grandchildren. I dreamed of the many ways I would wipe away her tears.

All my dreams dissolved into the reality of her death. She died young.

I slept through most of my lectures. I woke up in the late afternoons, took a shower, got dressed, and headed for any bar. My choice of bar depended on how much I intended to spend. Sometimes friends and acquaintances, whose tabs I had picked up on previous occasions, offered to pick up mine. I simply drank.

The first term of Year Two passed me by. How I was even able to take part in the term's examinations is a blur.

In the second term of Year Two, my tardiness to class and constant drunken binges were a concern only to me. I was in a world all by myself. The second term was also a blur. I just drank more.

By the third and final year of school, I decided to pull myself together—just enough to manage completing Year Two. I had begun attending lectures better than I previously did. Then something happened that got me into trouble with one "powerful" lecturer in my department.

We were having a holiday weekend. I was the last student to serve as the week's departmental student librarian; I had volunteered as part of my resolve to complete Year Two. I was no longer as concerned about my grades as I had been at the start of the school year.

As a result of the holiday weekend, I retreated into my safe hole—drinking. I forgot to place the key where it could be retrieved by lecturers needing access to the department's library. By the time the news reached me concerning the whereabouts of the library key, days had passed. This "powerful" lecturer almost burst a vein. He was so furious that he vowed to make whoever had the key pay heavily. He meant every word of his threat.

I got wind that he planned to take out his threat of retribution on every member of my class. That was when I summoned the willpower to visit him in his office. I apologized on behalf of my classmates. I told him the fault was entirely mine, and there was no need to mete out punishment to the whole class. I took responsibility and urged him to concentrate his displeasure only in my direction.

This lecturer carried out his threat. He frustrated an already frustrated me, who had no motivation for anything. He gave me failing grades in his courses, ensuring that I repeated the whole of Year Two. I was a Chemistry major; I needed both his courses to scale through.

This lecturer was bold and shameless enough to use white-out to scrub off my original grades and append whatever grades he considered punishment in line with his vow. He was truly a low-life lecturer.

On resumption of school for my second bite at Year Two, I seized the opportunity to mentor my new classmates. I had a successful second and third year. I graduated with honors, but by this time I had given up acting plays. I simply gave up on it. I detested the limelight. I still felt I had no reason to do anything meaningful; in fact, life had lost its meaning after the death of mummy.

I went about my education as a matter of routine. It was all very boring.

Second-bite Year Two was successful—no lecturer drama. I progressed to the final year.

Third year was a little better. I focused on studying, getting good enough grades to graduate, and leaving the university with a bachelor's degree. An interesting aspect of the requirements for a final-year Chemistry student to graduate was to submit a project work.

My supervisor for my project work was also working towards attaining a Ph.D. Project work required conducting experiments and sending samples of results overseas for analysis by well-equipped Chemistry laboratories. Samples from our department were always sent to Canada.

The analysis results from Canada and my results were not far off the mark. This earned me very good grades in my project work. I graduated with honors.

JOB HUNT

Where do I begin the story of my job hunting and attempts to settle down as an adult after obtaining an undergraduate degree and completing the mandatory one-year NYSC?

After organizing my friend's bachelor's party and the conclusion of his wedding ceremony in Kano, I returned to Zaria. I hung around with friends in Sabon Gari. I had been homeless since mummy died. All my three sisters were now married and raising families.

After the death of mummy, I was literally homeless. My friend's father, papa, had been consecrated Bishop and installed as the first Bishop of the newly created Kano Diocese of the Church of Nigeria, Anglican Communion. The old vicarage ceased to be our accommodation.

I devised a method to retain my university room by spending my vacation on campus. I had a very good rapport with the accommodation administration. Campus accommodation was always occupied year-round. Sometimes I would make a visit to Kano for a week, but the bulk of my vacation time I spent in the hostel.

This homelessness issue now reared its ugly head again. I had not made up my mind about which city or part of the country I was going to settle in.

Armed with the complimentary card I received when I visited Zaria towards the end of my service year, I began making trips to seek out the person I was supposed to introduce myself to. I was to show him the endorsed complimentary card. My friend—whose father had issued and endorsed the card for me to use in introducing myself— was also accommodating me temporarily in Zaria.

I made numerous trips to see this "big man," explained my situation, and expected him to guide me on how to obtain employment in the establishment where he was one of the managers. Instead, he regaled me with stories of his trips to numerous oil and gas–producing countries. After each meeting, he set up another appointment—always for the next time he was back in the country.

When I realized I was running out of funds traveling back and forth between Zaria and Kaduna, I decided to relocate to Kaduna.

ON THE MOVE

While in Kaduna, I met up with a group of acquaintances and former classmates. One of them offered me accommodation.

I kept showing up for my appointments, expecting that this man would assist me with employment. The back-and-forth continued until I finally realized that he was not going to help me—and he was not going to say so outright. He intended to wear down my patience. He succeeded, because I eventually gave up. I stopped going to his office.

To contribute to accommodation and upkeep while staying with my friend, I decided to work part-time. I accompanied him to the radio station where he worked. I was given the opportunity to write and participate in a radio drama to be aired once edited and certified fit for presentation.

Payment for this work was to be made after three months. I managed with the last funds in my savings. My friends and I shared whatever was available—for food, fun, and entertainment.

After about two months, I had a rethink. Job opportunities were few and scarce in Kaduna, and I was not prepared to take up just any kind of employment. I had my sights set higher.

One evening, while we were at the Press Club eating and drinking, I quietly informed my friends that I would be leaving Kaduna for good. They were not pleased that I was leaving the group, but I was leaving to seek greener pastures.

The next day, I wrote a letter of authorization requesting that my friend—who had introduced me to the radio station gig—collect on my behalf all monies due to me for work done. That was my contribution to the group in appreciation of their friendship and support.

I left Kaduna and journeyed to Benin City in the southern part of Nigeria.

The cousin I went to meet in Benin City had earlier offered to assist me in any way he could. He made this promise when he came on a condolence visit to Zaria from Lagos. He was devastated when he learned that mummy had passed.

He later relocated to Lagos to be closer to his grassroots. He was a retired banker who had gone into active grassroots politics.

When I arrived in Benin City, my cousin owned two properties side by side in the Government Reservation Area (GRA). One of the properties was rented to the Ministry of Defense, which allocated it to members of the armed forces for accommodation. The second property had an upper and a lower set of apartments. My cousin and his family occupied the upper floors, while the lower apartment was leased to the New Nigerian Bank and occupied by the bank's doctor.

I instantly hit it off with the New Nigerian Bank tenant, who happened to be a medical doctor and the official team doctor for the New Nigerian Bank Football Club of Benin City.

My sojourn in Benin City did not last very long. There were no job prospects. My cousin introduced me to a couple of people who made promises, but nothing materialized from them.

On one occasion, I was asked to submit an application to the Ministry of Water Resources in Benin City. I did, and I received assurances that I would be invited for a job interview. I waited for the call; the letter did not arrive for several weeks. When it eventually came, the interview date had already passed, and I was no longer in Benin City—I had relocated to Lagos.

I decided to head for Lagos. I had no permanent place of abode since mummy died. After graduation and throughout my NYSC days, I stayed away from close family members. I simply took care of my own affairs.

My immediate elder sister—the same one I stayed with during my exile to Kano, in whose house I lived while preparing for and writing my GCE examinations—now lived in Lagos with her family.

I began receiving messages expressing concern about my whereabouts and well-being. I left Benin City and headed straight to Lagos to see her. I was offered accommodation, albeit temporary.

I started job hunting in earnest. I had a clear idea of the kind of starter jobs I wanted. I was not prepared to settle for less than a management-in-training position. I wanted to get my foot in the door at a good level, one that would enhance my growth. I thought I had everything planned out. Life, however, had other lessons—strange, curious, bitter, and very painful lessons—to teach me.

My first experience with a corporate head-hunter was with a German national working for the Leventis Group of Companies. He held a Ph.D. degree and was a very effective head-hunter. I responded to one of the company's advertisements in the major Nigerian newspapers of that time, seeking university graduates interested in managerial positions. I applied and was invited for a first interview.

Fortunately, the interview took place at the company's head office, located at Iddo House, Iddo, Lagos.

All of us applicants for the interview were welcomed by a very tall, ramrod-straight man. He was the head-hunter. Discipline oozed from his pores; he carried the unmistakable aura of a no-nonsense individual.

He made it clear to all of us that this first interview was a "weeding exercise," intended to eliminate as many applicants as possible. We were instructed to listen to a recorded playback from a tape recorder, after which questions would follow. We were to mark our answers on provided sheets—multiple-choice format.

At the end of the exercise, we were ushered into a waiting area laden with snacks and drinks. We were told to await the results of the test we had just completed. After a while, we heard his loud, booming voice announcing that if your name was called, you should pack your things and leave—you had been eliminated.

Those of us whose names were not mentioned were asked to remain behind, help ourselves to the snacks and drinks, and await further instructions.

We were then ushered into a room for a one-on-one conversation with this giant of a man. He was quite friendly—very different from his earlier tone.

His conversation centered on my academic performance and my undergraduate major. Based on this, he determined that my next interview would take place in the northern state of Kano. I was to make my own travel arrangements, keep all receipts, and would be reimbursed at the conclusion of the entire process.

I was quite familiar with Kano. Our eldest sister and her family still resided there. I remembered that she and her family had thrown an impromptu party to celebrate my success in the GCE examinations on the day the results were published.

Three weeks after the first interview, I purchased a return plane ticket from Lagos to Kano and flew Nigerian Airways. The second interview was scheduled to take place at the Leventis headquarters in Kano.

This time, the process was similar: listening to a tape-recorded playback and answering questions. However, unlike the first interview, the answer sheets were not multiple-choice. Answers were to be written in short, concise sentences and, where necessary, brief paragraphs.

After the session, we were again ushered into a waiting room, also laden with snacks and drinks. We were allowed to help ourselves while waiting for our scripts to be graded.

Announcements were made by the head-hunter. Names that were called were eliminated and instructed to proceed to the accounts department to complete expense forms, produce receipts, and be reimbursed for their expenses.

Those of us who survived this stage were asked to wait behind for a one-on-one interaction with our recruiter.

I had my meeting with the doctor. Based on my qualifications, I was best suited for an opening in a town called Ughelli, a small town in the then Bendel State. Ughelli was home to Delta Glass Company, a division of the Leventis Group of Companies.

The same process applied—pay for your transportation and accommodation, keep all receipts, and at the end of the process, submit your claim for reimbursement. By this time, my receipts were piling up, and I was still in the "race."

After Kano, I used my return ticket to get back to Lagos—my temporary base, or so I thought. From Lagos, I boarded public transportation to Warri, a city I had heard many stories about but had never visited. From Warri, I took a taxi to Ughelli.

On the drive to Ughelli, I focused on looking out the window, stealing quick glances on both sides of the road. I heaved a sigh of relief when I spotted the Delta Glass factory along the road. Shortly after passing the factory, I saw a hotel and asked the driver to stop. I alighted. I guessed I had arrived at my destination for the night.

I checked into the hotel. Dinner had already been served, but I pleaded for a quick meal to be prepared for me. After my meal—which I ate via room service—I turned on the air conditioner to create a very cold environment. I set my bedside alarm to ensure I did not oversleep. The interview was scheduled for the next morning.

The following morning, I took a taxi to the interview venue. The process was straightforward: upon arrival at the company gate, you identified yourself and were directed to the administration department.

When I arrived at the admin department, I met other interviewees already seated and waiting. I sat down and joined them.

A white man came out to address us all—this time a different one. I guessed the doctor had completed his part of the head-hunting process, which involved the first and second interviews.

We were led through the company yard to the company's clubhouse. The clubhouse presented a pleasant view: a well-kept lawn, a lawn tennis court, a swimming pool, a pond with ducks swimming leisurely, and other recreational facilities. We were seated at and around the bar.

This stage of the interview involved general discussion. We were being observed and graded by onlookers—hiring managers of the company. The majority of them were people we would understudy and eventually take over from if hired. We were being prepared for roles as trainee technical managers.

These onlookers sat strategically around us during the interviews. Their job was to listen to our pitch, our tone, and the soundness of our discussions. The lead interviewer would introduce a topic—either as a question or a general statement—and we, the interviewees, were to engage in a healthy discussion. All the while, we were being watched and graded.

Different forms of this process continued, and eliminations were carried out at various stages. I continued to survive until only six of us applicants were left. At this stage, I did not know how many trainee technical managers the company intended to hire.

The final stage, involving the six of us, required visits to four offices. In each office sat a manager. We were to knock and enter at our appointed times. A roster showing the offices and the specific times each of us was to visit was handed to us.

The first office I visited belonged to a young-looking white man with a pleasant smile plastered on his face and a firm handshake. We chatted about our days in the university and university courses. He explained his job, the role of a trainee technical manager, and what was expected of new hires. He was very encouraging and reassuring.

The next room had a similar ambience, occupied by a slightly older white man. He offered more insight into job requirements and expectations, along with further encouragement and reassurance that I was on the right track. By this time, I was already feeling good.

At the third office, I knocked, and the voice that ushered me in was not that of a white man—or any foreigner for that matter—but that of a Nigerian, a black man from Ughelli. I later learned he was standing in for a white man who had been called away on a family emergency.

The man behind the desk did not seem comfortable with his handshake. He generally looked bored, and there was condescension in his voice—he was condescending.

After the handshake and introductions, he asked a pointed question that caught me off guard. I recovered without batting an eyelid. His question was, "Don't you think you should be pursuing a master's degree instead of applying for a manager's position?" He added, "I think you are too young. You should go back to school for a master's degree."

I politely replied to him, "What if I am a product of a communal effort to send me to study and obtain a bachelor's degree? What if my community expects me to start work and pay that scholarship forward?"

He was not buying whatever I was explaining. One glance at my young and handsome face convinced him that I was too young to join the company as a manager. My time was up with this man. I immediately regretted meeting him.

By the time I knocked on the fourth and final door and was ushered in by a burly white man with a friendly, broad smile on his face, I could still taste the bile in my mouth from the previous encounter with the Ughelli man.

After the last office visit, we were all ushered into the waiting room. Only two people were asked to stay behind. I was among the four that were let go. It was already late at night. I returned to my hotel room dejected.

I could not sleep that night. My mind kept replaying all the perks that came with the job I had just lost.

The Leventis Group of Companies, upon hire, offered a choice of either a Renault or a Mercedes-Benz vehicle, appliances to furnish an apartment located in the staff quarters, access to the staff club, and more. Payments were deducted from each pay check until the car and home appliances were fully paid for.

What would life have looked like—with a young me driving a Renault 18T and living in a fully furnished house in a reserved area of town, bordered by a staff club? That was the life—the life I dreamed of. A life one man extinguished by asking a foolish interview question and making unhealthy assumptions. I blamed the Ughelli man for my misfortune. I swore at him in my sleep.

The next morning, I went to the admin department, completed my expense forms, presented my receipts, and was handed a handsome sum of money—more than a month's salary of a Level 10 civil servant at the time. It was good money.

I journeyed to Benin City and visited a classmate from my university days. We had studied together for our final examinations in Year Three. He was my course mate, a true Benin boy.

My friend received me warmly and was genuinely happy to see me. After reminiscing about our last days of studying and writing exams, I told him about my job-hunting experiences so far.

He explained that there were little to no employment opportunities in Benin City. I told him I would be heading for Lagos—that was where I hoped things would finally happen.

I ended up spending the weekend with him in Benin City. We partied—nightclubs, dancing, drinking, visiting pepper-soup joints—and generally lived it up. My friend's father had passed on but left him and his siblings some inheritance. My friend was hardly ever broke.

After the weekend frolicking, I expected the disappointment of missing out on my dream job to dissipate. It did not. There was a heavy ache in my heart that I carried around.

I headed back to Lagos with a promise to invite my friend over if I found job opportunities to share with him. We promised to remain in constant communication. My Benin City friend eventually relocated to Lagos.

In Lagos, I continued my job search, looking for opportunities with the kind of prospects I dreamed of—jobs where I could learn, grow on the job, and eventually rise to the very top. I trusted my ability and capability to adapt; I was a fast learner.

Submitting applications eventually became almost a full-time job on its own. I started sensing rejection, with prospects dimming by the day.

One day, I overheard a conversation concerning my job hunt. The people involved were questioning my seriousness about getting a job. I had maintained my habit of enjoying the good things of life. The money I received after my debacle in Ughelli and the trainee manager interview was still keeping me afloat.

They even insinuated that all I wanted was a "manager's job." I owed no one any apology—that was the level at which I wanted to start my life. Then, subtle suggestions in the form of advice were thrown my way: I should apply for a teaching job. The Lagos State Government had just embarked on a massive drive to recruit graduate teachers for its secondary school system.

I decided to visit the teacher recruitment center in Lagos. A sea of heads—tired-looking applicants with copies of their CVs tucked into long brown envelopes—waited under the Lagos heat and humidity.

When I finally managed to meander through the crowd and get close enough to hear and follow instructions on how to proceed with the recruitment exercise, it became clear that science teachers were in particularly high demand.

Something very strange happened to me. A woman I had never seen or met in my life approached me and asked to see copies of my documents. I showed them to her. She took the copies and told me she would be back. I never saw her again.

Not too long after she "disappeared," I was surprised to hear my name called among others. I was ushered into a room—I presumed it was the interview room. I was asked to show my identification, after which I submitted two passport-sized photographs. Right there and then, I was issued a letter of appointment and assigned to a school, with instructions to resume the following Monday at my duty post.

I never heard from or laid eyes on that "mysterious" woman again—ever.

When I arrived home to my accommodation in Lagos, my hosts were happy that I had finally secured a job. On the other hand, I was not too pleased. I considered this employment merely a stepping stone toward my desired dream job.

After resuming my new position, I discovered that science teachers were highly sought after. I settled down and assumed the role of senior Chemistry teacher at the school.

Since I had promised my Benin City friend and former classmate that once any job opportunity arose in Lagos I would send for him, I immediately did so. He promptly left Benin City for Lagos.

Upon arrival, he took up accommodation with a friend who was working with one of the federal security agencies at the time. My friend was employed as a science teacher and resumed duties immediately. I was pleased that I had fulfilled my promise to him.

The Lagos State Schools Management Board required all newly recruited teachers to report to their local school board offices for identification and verification, to prevent infiltration of the payroll by fictitious "ghost" workers. Instantly, I recalled my experience working at the construction site in Kano, where site supervisors colluded with payroll clerks to create ghost workers. I smiled to myself. Greed, I thought, is the same everywhere.

During the verification exercise, I stood alone quietly smoking a cigarette—a habit I had cultivated in my final year at St. Paul's College, Wusasa, Zaria. As I enjoyed my nicotine, I felt a gentle tap on my shoulder. Another smoker, desperate to light his cigarette from the tip of mine, introduced himself. After lighting up, we struck up a conversation. He asked if we could be friends. I said, *why not*.

We became friends—and later colleagues—teaching in the same school. He taught Fine Arts.

My newfound friend and teaching colleague and I began to spend more time together after the day's work was done. We smoked a lot of cigarettes and drank a lot. He lived with his parents, but his accommodation was a separate apartment building behind the main house where his parents lived.

Sometimes—mostly on Fridays—we crawled the town, nightclubbing all night. My Benin City friend, now also in Lagos, often joined us. I started staying away from my accommodation. This behavior upset my hosts, who assumed I was frittering away my pay.

The school board had a policy of not paying new hires during the first three months of employment. New employees received their first pay check after three months—a cumulative payment for that period. I was banking on this bulk pay as a down payment to rent an apartment of my own, or at least to team up with someone to share one. The pressure was mounting, albeit subtly, for me to give my hosts their space.

Now that I was in Lagos, some form of relationship-building began with my father—yes, my father. I tried to build a relationship with him, but I felt his new family—a wife and three boys—were much more his focus.

For reasons I still cannot fully understand, he pleaded with me one day after I mentioned that I had not yet received any pay and would not until after three months, when the cumulative pay check would be issued. I also mentioned that this money would serve as my deposit to secure my own accommodation.

My father pleaded with me that when I received the three months' pay check, I should lend him the entire sum. He promised to pay me back with interest as soon as his gratuity was released—he had just retired from work.

When I received my first-ever salary as a graduate, I handed it all over to my father. To this day, I cannot fathom how or why I made that decision.

Needless to say, I do not know whether he already knew, at the time he made the request, that he would not repay the money.

He did not pay me back. He never did. I asked him on two occasions. He made excuses and promised to pay, but he never did—ever. I never asked him again, nor did I ever discuss the matter with him afterward.

Meanwhile, tension had been brewing with my hosts. It eventually came to a head. We quarreled, yelled at each other, and my mummy's sister was called from Zaria to Lagos to intervene. She urged me to move out. I heeded her advice. I moved out.

I had nowhere to go. No accommodation. My friends did not own places of their own, and I had no down payment to rent my own place or share an apartment with flatmates.

When you are desperate and faced with no options, there will always be a way—no matter how crazy. I moved my "office." I emptied a couple of chemical storage lockers in the science laboratory, stuffed my pillows and blankets into one locker, and my suitcase into another.

At night, I would discreetly open the laboratory, lay blankets on the large tables, place my pillows, and sleep. Mosquitoes had a field day feasting on my blood. I had to light mosquito-repellent coils.

I woke up very early and ran across to a building opposite the laboratory. This building was formerly the school dormitory when missionaries administered the school. There was no longer a boarding system; the state government now ran secondary school day-wise. The building had been converted into shared accommodation for teachers, especially Ghanaian nationals who had escaped economic hardship in their country to fill the teacher shortage in Nigerian schools. I used the bathrooms there for my morning clean-up. Then I proceeded to resume my duties. I also used the laboratory as my office.

One day, an acquaintance of mine from university days sought me out. He drove to my workplace in his light-blue Volkswagen Beetle. We chatted about our school days, and he eventually broached the issue of accommodation. He said he had nowhere to sleep. I almost laughed out loud—I had accommodation of my own.

He explained that he had quarreled with his father, a retired army officer, and had been thrown out. I was curious. We had not been particularly close in university; we mostly met at parties and drinking joints.

I explained my situation and sleeping arrangements. To my surprise, he latched onto the idea immediately. He wanted, straightaway, to be my "squatting mate."

Now I had a companion. The mosquitoes could feast on two people instead of one. At least I would get some relief while they busied themselves with the new "inmate."

We made ourselves as comfortable as we could under the circumstances. I provided toiletries, food, and sometimes paid for cigarettes for both of us. My fellow squatter was broke—very broke. If I needed him to give me a ride, I bought fuel for his car. On occasion, I even paid for tire replacements.

My friend—the one who had asked to light his cigarette from the tip of mine while we were waiting to be validated by our local education board, my colleague who taught Fine

Arts—had put his girlfriend in the family way. He still lived with his parents, and his father was quite strict about such matters.

He sought my advice, but I was preparing to travel to the eastern part of Nigeria—precisely the state where I had served my NYSC. He told me his father had given him an ultimatum: either marry his girlfriend or move out of the house. His father was willing to throw him out if he refused to marry the woman he had impregnated.

I promised to support him, whatever choice he made. I knew he was not willing to lose his accommodation or damage his relationship with his parents, yet he was unsure if he was ready for marriage. He sounded desperate. I consoled him and told him that when I returned from my trip, we would look at the options more carefully and make a good decision.

This trip was undertaken at the request of my former host—before we quarreled and I moved out of his home, ending up sleeping on tables in my office. He wanted me to contact some bankers. He was an erudite banker, very knowledgeable and good at his job. He gave me enough funds to cover my transport and hotel accommodation.

After completing my assignment and before heading back to Lagos, I stopped to visit my friend at the school where I had served my NYSC primary assignment. We had lunch and talked about our relationship. She reiterated that in their tradition, her parents had no say in her choice of spouse; it was the elders of the family who decided. Being the only daughter, she would not be allowed to marry any man outside her tribe. That was an unwritten law.

As much as she would have wanted the relationship to continue, that was as far as it could go. We parted ways on very good terms.

THE MAKING OF US

On my return from that trip, my friend was already planning his wedding. His pregnant girlfriend was now far gone in her pregnancy. His father was breathing down his neck, he was broke and could not afford a place of his own, and he needed to retain the apartment in his father's house. He made up his mind to respect his father's wishes and marry his pregnant girlfriend.

Once he made his decision known, his family contributed funds to help him acquire an apartment of his own.

My friend mentioned me as his best man, and I immediately proceeded to organize a bachelor's party in preparation for the forthcoming wedding. His newly acquired accommodation was the ideal place to host the party. It was an all-nighter, and the following day was the wedding.

The wedding was scheduled to take place at the courthouse in City Hall, with the reception to follow at the then Gulf Club House. Gulf Oil Company was one of the very big players in the oil industry in Nigeria at the time, and my friend's father-in-law was a very senior manager in the company. He had access to the company's clubhouse.

After the courthouse marriage ceremony, the bridal train moved on to the reception venue. We were kept in a private waiting room, and the bride's father arranged that we be served whatever we requested. I observed that the bride and groom, the bridesmaid, and myself—the best man—all smoked cigarettes profusely, even the pregnant bride.

I found myself attracted to the chief bridesmaid, for the rather silly reason that she smoked and drank as much as I did. I was waiting for an opportunity with her later.

After the reception, there was an after-wedding party at the bride's father's home. We were all present for the night-long celebration. By then, I had already had quite a few drinks and was in a very good mood.

During the party at the "night party," the groom was able to extricate himself from the activities going on around him and come have a smoke. Suddenly, he remembered that his bride had a close friend next door he wanted me to meet. We moved next door briefly, he introduced me to his wife's friend, and the first thing that came out of my mouth was, "I am going to marry you." She smiled and said nothing.

I noticed her small voice and very slim size. I fell for her instantly, but I harbored a doubt; she looked like she might be too young for me. At the time, I did not know she was only two years younger than I am. I liked her instantly, but by then the chief bridesmaid and I were already in a kind of "hide and seek" game. She was taunting me, and I was on to her.

Whenever she noticed I was having a discussion with the lady next door at the night party, she would come close to light her cigarette, and I would scurry away to be by her side. We exchanged some banter, she would leave, and I would go back to continue my discussion. I played this game of jumping from one discussion to the other.

While I was away on one of my chit-chats with the chief bridesmaid, I noticed a cluster of men around "my wife." I quickly broke into the circle and told all the men to leave. I declared boldly that they should not be having a conversation with my wife. The men laughed; she just smiled. I was serious, and the men dispersed.

I did not pursue my interest in "my wife" after that night. I had one or two encounters with the bridesmaid. In our first encounter after the wedding ceremonies, she told me that she actually liked older men—men older than I was at that time. At our second encounter, however, I noticed a thawing on her part, and she was showing a lot more interest. I, on the other hand, after the thrill of playing hide and seek, and with a clearer mind devoid of the influence of alcohol, was less interested in any relationship with her.

The start of anything between us ended after that encounter. I did not push further.

On the other hand, one afternoon, about a month and some after the wedding, my friend, the groom, brought to my notice that his wife had put to bed a bouncing baby girl— what a thrill. He wanted me to accompany him to his in-laws and thereafter to break the news to his wife's friend, her parents' next-door neighbor, my "wife." I was okay with going to her in-laws and apprehensive about a visit to his wife's friend. I had not seen her since the last time—the night I made my bold declaration, proclaiming her my wife in public and scaring away all others.

After visiting his parents-in-law and breaking the good news, we proceeded next door, a party of four young men. My "wife" welcomed us nicely with a smile, but I noticed that when she looked at me, there was a glint in her eyes. I was quiet, because the guilt of not following up on my bluster on the night of the wedding ceremonies weighed heavily on my mind.

She asked each of the three in our party of four what they would like to be offered as refreshments; she did not ask me. But when the drinks arrived, she served me exactly what I was drinking on the day we were first introduced. My mind registered this detail. She was very much interested in me. She was noticing things about me, including my taste in alcohol.

In my mind, I was thinking that this poor lady did not know she was falling for a "homeless" guy. I had no place of my own. We delivered the good news that her friend had put to bed safely, a daughter. She was very happy, after which we were ready to depart.

I then requested to pay her a visit very soon, and not to wait until some other event before seeing her again. She reassured me that I was welcome to visit her anytime, and that I did not need to give any notice of my visit. That was very reassuring.

I visited her every day, spent my evenings with her, then retired to my office cum bedroom. I was still squatting in my office.

After a while, I let her know that I was homeless and looking for accommodation—that my office, the school's laboratory, doubled as my bedroom, and that I had a roommate, a fellow squatter.

Opposite the school's laboratory, there was a single-story building with a set of rooms. On the left side of the building, on both floors, were single-bedroom self-contained suites, one on each floor. Both were occupied, and so were the single rooms.

One day, the tenants in the upper-floor self-contained suite moved out; they had found accommodation outside the school premises. I promptly moved into the accommodation without making a request or being granted permission to do so.

I had broken a series of rules. I did not consult the principal of the main school, the custodian of the accommodation. I did not submit any application for accommodation. I did not even belong to any accommodation waiting list. The race to eject me from the accommodation began in earnest.

The teacher who had been on the waiting list "forever" was aggrieved and came constantly to plead with me to vacate the accommodation. The principal, the custodian, fired a series of warning letters in my direction, some carrying threats of forcible ejection. I remained adamant. I was enjoying my newfound accommodation. I now invited my "wife," who visited and brought cooked meals with her. Things were looking upward—until the threats of forceful eviction began to look like reality.

After a while, I moved out and went back to squatting.

After I vacated the accommodation, I had illegally assumed, a room in the main building became vacant. Another teacher left for a bigger apartment outside the school premises. I formally made a request for the room, and it was granted.

Now, I legally owned a room in the school's compound. Deductions were made from my monthly pay cheque as rent. My squatter moved with me into this one room. My squatter friend now had a job but was yet to receive any salary. I still paid for everything—toiletries and food. It was now a decent accommodation, better than sleeping on laboratory tables.

By this time, my "wife" and I had agreed to be boyfriend and girlfriend officially. My girlfriend travelled home to see her parents and spend Christmas. We had met in October of that year, and we were less than three months into our relationship. I had become used to spending a lot of time with her.

So, her travelling out of town left me with a lot of time on my hands. I ate my meals mostly in two places. One of those places was across from my accommodation, not too far from my girlfriend's. There, after my meal, I would take my time to wind down with a bottle or two of beer and smoke some cigarettes. I lingered, and sometimes my squatter joined me for meals and drinks. I picked up the tabs, always.

One Sunday afternoon, I walked into this joint and saw my squatter before he saw me. I made my way to a table hidden from him and watched him. He ordered a sumptuous meal, was smoking, and ordering drinks for himself. On Sundays, he did not work, and on Sundays the banks did not open for business. These were days before ATMs. You wanted money from your bank account? Simple—you went to the bank, queued up, and saw the teller for all your transactions.

My squatter was ordering a sumptuous meal and washing it down with bottles of beer. Yet he had not received any payment for work going back more than three months. He did not spend money because he did not have any.

After my meal and drinks, I paid my bill and then sauntered over to where my squatter was seated. The look on his face was priceless; it was as if he had just encountered a ghost. His big eyeballs were popping out of their sockets, and he started to stammer in an attempt to proffer an explanation for the sudden "wealth."

I sat opposite him and reassured him to take things easy. I noticed a box containing two pairs of shoes—very beautiful and expensive-looking shoes. He was already about to explain the source of the shoes. I did not say anything negative to him; I only said, "See you later," and left for our shared accommodation.

When he finally arrived home, he told me he had just met a new lady who ran a catering business. She bought him the two pairs of expensive, good-looking shoes and gave him some pocket money to spend. She wanted him to look good. I congratulated him on his good fortune.

Not long after my coincidental run-in with my squatter roommate, where he was living the dream—eating and drinking all by himself—he decided to move out. He was going to live with his newfound lady friend. I wished him luck. I was now living alone, in my one-room apartment in the school accommodation for teachers.

My "wife," who was now my girlfriend, began to visit freely. Our relationship continued to grow. She returned from her trip to visit her parents after the Christmas and New Year celebrations. Her birthday came up in the middle of the year, in June, and I decided to throw a birthday party to celebrate her. I ordered a goat from the school's yard keeper, who tended goats for sale. We enjoyed a variety of food, especially goat-meat pepper soup, and, of course, lots and lots of drinks.

As I had declared the first time I set my eyes on my girlfriend—that she was my "wife"—I meant every word of it. So, when we visited our doctor's office to carry out a series of tests about a month after her birthday party, and the doctor confirmed that we were expecting a baby, a lot of events began to happen simultaneously.

First, we broke the news to family and friends. The news reached my girlfriend's parents back home. She was summoned to bring me to see them. I did so after consulting my family members. I took with me the first drinks, as required by tradition. You do not visit your in-laws empty-handed.

Our visit to my girlfriend's parents was very interesting in many ways. I was welcomed with open arms and treated as a member of the family right away. I immediately started referring to both her parents as papa and mama. We were told to commence plans to get married, as we both agreed in their presence that we were committed to each other.

Both mama and papa were less interested in my financial standing, nor were they concerned that I was only a secondary school teacher. They were concerned only that we cared for each other enough to want to spend the rest of our lives together.

We were introduced in the month of October in one year, and by December of the following year we were married—both in the traditional way and in holy matrimony in a Catholic cathedral. I was raised an Anglican and got married a Catholic.

A one-week honeymoon was spent in Benin City. An uncle of mine provided us accommodation, and another provided a vehicle and a driver. At the end of our one-week honeymoon, our driver drove us straight to our one-room apartment in the school compound, where we began our married life in earnest.

Soon after, as we were settling into married life, we were blessed with the best and greatest gift ever. We welcomed our first-born child, our son, and our joy.

We were now a family of three, residing in our one-bedroom apartment. Neither my wife nor I complained; we simply made plans to secure a better and more secure accommodation.

The quest for new accommodation was accelerated by the wicked and heartless act of the principal of the main school, who doubled as our landlord. Our son's clothes, hanging on a clothesline to air-dry, were snatched away by agents of the "landlord." He believed that we should not be hanging clothes on the clothesline, claiming it was not good for the aesthetics of the building. That was merely an excuse to foment trouble; he was still angry from my earlier confrontation with him over the allocation of accommodation.

After a heated argument, he returned the seized clothes. My wife and I agreed not to dress our precious son in any of the returned items. We made a bonfire of all the clothes and burned them.

At this point, it became imperative to find accommodation outside the school premises. We finally secured a three-room apartment. This accommodation was a fresh breath of air after more than a year-long feud with our former "landlord."

RED HERRINGS AND HARD ROADS

The landlady of our new accommodation was very friendly and accommodating. She relied on our advice on how to keep her property clean, safe, and maintain respect among the different families renting from her. We assisted her in doing just that. We remained in this accommodation, as we later discovered, for too long—longer than necessary. That is life.

I do not know whether it is my personal belief, an African thing, or simply a human expectation that when you get married, have a child or children, and change accommodation, things begin to get better—life starts to take shape, and you are favored.

Taking up teaching was only a stopgap, as I had my sights set on very "good" jobs—well-paid jobs leading to a fulfilling career. This was not forthcoming. Instead, a series of strange patterns began to emerge in the course of my job search.

The first incident I noticed was during a crowded, all-out federal government recruitment exercise into the Federal Civil Service. I was interested in the Federal Ministry of Health, hoping to pursue a career in rural water resources development, and I also applied to the Federal Ministry of Water Resources.

Many of us applicants arrived at the recruitment venue very early. By early evening, however, my name had not been called. There were no cell phones at that time, and I was anxious to know how my wife and son were faring—there was no news. I was hungry, tired, and frustrated with the slow pace of activities.

A couple of hours later, I assumed the interviews would be called off for the day and resumed the next day. I decided to leave for home—to eat, see my young family, and get refreshed for what I believed would be the following day. I was wrong.

No sooner had I left than my name was announced over the public address system. The announcement was repeated continuously. The report I later received was that the interview panel urgently needed to see me. Unfortunately for me, I was long gone. The Federal Civil Service turned out to be one of the most "lucrative" workplaces in the country. I missed out on that opportunity.

I was interviewed twice by a federal government parastatal with oversight under the Ministry of Oil and Gas. On both occasions, the person I believed was helping me secure employment only sold me a red herring. Their intention was to create the illusion of assistance.

As this hit-and-miss pattern continued, the same kind of red herring assistance followed me year after year. For about three consecutive years, offers were made to help me gain admission into an MBA program. That, too, turned out to be an illusion. There were even offers to pay for admission forms. All of it was merely a simulation of help—nothing more.

There was some genuine advice from a friend who, at the time, worked as a manager in a frozen fish distribution company. He was interested in improving himself and moving on to something bigger. He had the right connections at a university—one of the first-generation universities. I was to accompany him; we were both going to be admitted into the university's MBA program. We applied and were invited for interview. I consciously made the choice not to attend.

The university was out of town, and I could not leave my young family to go away for studies. It was a painful decision, but I stood by it. I declined the interview. My friend was successful; he completed the course and later changed career. He became a banker of repute.

In the meantime, a pattern of attending interviews emerged in my life. Almost all applications I submitted resulted in calls for interviews, yet none led to employment. It was frustrating—very frustrating.

Five years after our first child, our son, we were blessed with a second child, our precious little daughter. It was a period of struggle. We were very happy about this addition to our family. She had the biggest and brightest eyes, and her smiles were earth-shaking—magical.

My struggle to find a suitable job had by now taken a heavy toll. I took up teaching private science classes to make ends meet. My wife worked as a front office administrator in an insurance broking firm. We still struggled financially, but we hoped things would change. I suspect that many people around us took delight in our struggles. Those who were in a position to offer assistance either refused to lift a finger or simply dangled red herrings.

Ten years into my teaching career—after five years in my first school—I was transferred to another school. I was in my fifth year at the second school when the military administration announced that civil servants who had completed ten years of service or more could retire from government service. I took the advice to retire.

I was going to retire—and do what? I had no idea what I was retiring into. I was still relatively young for retirement. I saw it as a way to disengage myself from a job I had taken up as a stepping stone, a job that had now lasted ten years. I had to eject myself from it. I did just that. I retired after ten years.

At the time I retired, my wife had also left her employment. We were both jobless. I retired because I felt that if I did not get out of the job, I would remain in it for the rest of my life. I wanted none of that. I received flak from everyone with an opinion—not that those who opposed my "retirement" offered any assistance or were prepared to do so later. No. They simply weaponized my voluntary retirement against me.

I struggled through and overcame all the red tape required to secure my lump-sum entitlement as a retiree, after agreeing to the terms laid down by the civil servant in charge. I needed the money to pay for a shop space located within trekking distance of our accommodation. The shop was strategically located.

The amount collected as retirement benefits, combined with some of our savings, paid for the shop space, furniture, and equipment. The equipment consisted of a manual typewriter (a Triumph model), an electric typewriter, and a Z-60 photocopier—not suited for commercial purposes. We did not know any better at the time.

We set up shop. A family of four—my wife, our son, our daughter, and myself—relied on these three pieces of equipment for our upkeep. This was more than risk-taking; it bordered on the realm of crazy expectation and hope— hope that something would break through for us. We had a very long wait ahead of us.

I had earlier been introduced to my cousin's younger brother when he was still resident in Lagos, before he moved his family to Benin City. When I was in Benin City job-seeking, this younger cousin—distinguished from his elder brother—was studying at the university there.

He had since completed his studies and the mandatory one-year NYSC. He was now back in Lagos, living with his sister and her family, and also looking for a befitting job. He spent considerable time looking in the wrong direction, seeking assistance to gain entry into one of the Lagos State government parastatals in the Ministry of Information.

My younger cousin later recalled a conversation he once had with his elder brother. He told me that in that conversation, his brother said that if he ever needed wise counsel, he should endeavor to stay close to me, because I would always offer wise counsel. My cousin's elder brother was right.

After searching endlessly and appearing at the office of the ADC to the then Lagos State military administrator—enduring numerous promises, none of which had materialized—my younger cousin sought me out in Lagos.

After he related his ordeal of job searching, I reminded him that because of our lack of very strong connections, I would advise him to pick up a teaching job. This was all before I retired, and I assured him that I would ensure he did not remain in teaching for long. He approached an ADC to the governor who was his schoolmate. The ADC was pleased to grant his request, and he obtained a teaching appointment the same day. It was difficult for the ADC to fix him up with any other job; those were reserved for more "connected" persons.

At the time, I was running an extra science after-school program for which I charged a fee. I introduced my younger cousin to teach English classes, and I paid him monthly, exactly according to the number of students in his class. The money he earned was used for transportation. He was teaching and simultaneously attending a master's degree program at the University of Lagos.

In the course of his master's program, he was privileged to meet some top civil servants already well established in the civil service. He became very close to a particular classmate. They studied together, completed assignments together, grew close, and eventually became very good friends.

That was the path I had in mind when I advised my younger cousin to take up a teaching job and enroll in a master's program. He was initially skeptical, having just entered into a shared accommodation arrangement with a former high school classmate. It was through this arrangement that I was introduced to his flatmate, who later became my friend. This was the same friend who introduced me to the MBA program I could not attend—he attended successfully and later became a banker.

My younger cousin's friendship with his course mate blossomed. His friend eventually introduced him to the head of one of the parastatals in the Federal Ministry of Aviation, and he was offered a job appointment. This became the greatest turning point in my younger cousin's life.

My younger cousin's new appointment came with training outside Nigeria, scheduled after a probationary period. He was eventually sent for the training, and we all waited with bated breath for this opportunity. We survived a false alarm scare concerning this much-anticipated move. Training "abroad" connotes estacode—monies paid to the trainee in "hard" currencies. In most cases, this money signifies the beginning of getting out of "poverty."

We prayed and fasted for this opportunity. After the initial scare, he was finally scheduled for the training. He went for six months and saved almost all of his estacode. With those savings, he purchased a vehicle—part of the expected and anticipated outcome of the trip abroad.

Another anticipated move was starting a business together—my younger cousin and I. I was "retired" and had a lot of time on my hands, so I could monitor and manage our business. The outcome of this anticipated move, however, was disappointment—disappointment based on some "wise counsel" that relatives should not be involved in business partnerships, because such partnerships never end well. I was never given the opportunity to disprove that line of thought. On account of this counsel, my younger cousin and I did not go ahead with that decision after his return from abroad.

I simply chalked it down to life. Life had happened again.

Thereafter, I began to notice that ideas and advice I gave to my younger cousin, during discussions he might be having within a group, were sometimes praised—but the credit for those ideas or advice was given to someone else. I simply laughed it off. It amused me, as I could not fathom the reason for any of it.

I continued managing the three pieces of equipment in my shop, and we continued to survive—myself, my wife, and our two beautiful, wonderful, and well-behaved children. I must state emphatically that we ate very well. Our home never lacked love or very good food. We kept an open door of sharing in our good meals. Anyone and everyone who ever visited our humble abode will testify to having shared plates of sumptuous food with us. It remains our culture to this day.

In between seeing the children off to school and being present to receive them when they returned, I spent time visiting my younger cousin at his office. He was now fully established in his workplace. I was introduced to his colleagues, and I became a regular presence there, in anticipation of an opportunity for a breakthrough.

What looked like the beginning of something came from a side gig my younger cousin and his colleagues were involved in—a completely legitimate undertaking. On one occasion, they needed my proficiency in speaking one of the local Nigerian languages. I was to convince their immediate boss, who also spoke the language. I carried out the assignment successfully and was adequately compensated.

I saw this as an opening to my anticipated breakthrough. I convinced the three of us to register a business name, using my shop address as our business address. We did so and even went as far as engaging a lawyer for the process. We held an elaborate opening meeting at the Lagos Sheraton Hotel, which ended with a buffet and drinks.

Our company was now established, with the sharing formula discussed and accepted. The legitimate side gig continued, and by agreement, my participation was minimal, and so was my percentage cut at this stage. If our clients felt obliged to move their business to the next stages, then my participation would grow, as I would be involved with commitments outside my partners' workplace. The more I was involved, the more my share of the cut would increase.

On our first real deal, the initial part of the business was concluded, and my share was given to me. The next levels, I believed, would bring the breakthrough I so badly needed. Our client was very pleased with the first steps and called us to a meeting. At the meeting, our client virtually granted us a blank cheque. He instructed his adviser, who liaised with our team, to provide us with whatever we required for the next steps. He even offered us a weekend getaway to brainstorm. He wanted a simplified version of the document our business had prepared for him.

To my utter shock and disbelief, during our debriefing after the meeting with the client, my business partners declined to go on with the client's demands. Both of them not only turned down the weekend getaway, they also turned down any chance of doing anything further. As far as they were concerned, they had successfully delivered on their agreement to prepare a document that would pass muster, and that was the end of it. If the client wanted to proceed further, he would have to do so without "our" input.

I pleaded with my business partners. I told them this was the breakthrough I might have been waiting for, and that, per our agreement, moving forward would work to my advantage. Clearly, they had already made up their minds even before the big meeting with our client. The reason they gave was that they now had a new director. The director was watching everybody's moves, and as civil servants, they were not prepared to be caught in any serious trouble. I reminded both of them that they were not doing anything illegal.

My thought at the time was that they were content with whatever they were earning from simply writing documents that helped clients obtain licenses. They were not interested in how the client utilized the license afterward.

I was not sure they were concerned about—or even cared how—their decision affected me, financially or emotionally. Their minds were already made. They had to protect their civil service jobs.

I was stunned beyond words. My emotions rose. I sat quietly and sipped beer, one bottle after another. Ox-tail pepper soup lost its taste. My appetite was gone.

After this monumental disappointment, I drastically reduced my appearances at my business partners' office. I did not want to be the reason they might get sanctioned or even lose their jobs.

Another very strange occurrence followed—one that still baffles me to this day. Around this time, there had been some form of reconciliation with my sister and her family. If you recall, we had earlier quarreled, which led to my leaving their home. Her husband introduced me to the general manager, a white man, of a new bank situated in Ikoyi, Lagos.

The bank was operating from a rented building. Office space was constrained; even the general manager's office was tiny. He invited me for an interview, which turned into more of a meet-and-greet. I sat across from him in his cramped office. We talked about many things, and I sensed that he liked my intellect and my person. He mentioned that the bank was close to completing a move to a new location— a building they owned, not far from their current premises.

The general manager told me he was looking for a personal assistant, someone with a public-relations angle to liaise between him, as GM, and the PR department. He felt I fit the bill. He promised to contact me upon his return from the United Kingdom. He was travelling for a two-week vacation before resuming office in the new building.

He never returned. During an evening stroll at a London train station, he kicked his toe against an obstruction, fell, and was pronounced dead. He neither returned to Nigeria nor resumed office in the new building. He was gone—and so was my anticipated breakthrough from joblessness. I began to question this series of misfortunes.

After every disappointment, I simply picked myself up and looked forward to another opportunity. One soon presented itself. One of our neighbors—whose shop was next to the one my wife ran with the help of an employee, as I had now become more of a hunter of opportunities— invited my wife and me to their home. It was her husband's birthday, and she was throwing a party for him.

We attended the party in one of the lovely parts of Lagos. Her husband had just retired from one of the biggest oil companies operating in Nigeria at the time. The lady introduced us to her husband, and later he expressed a desire to discuss a business opportunity with me—a welcome development. We fixed an appointment for the next day. His new office was situated within a section of his sprawling home.

He explained his line of business to me, which included wood export—the export of timber, especially teak wood, to Asia, particularly India, and to Europe, especially Italy. He was having difficulty getting anything past the Nigerian ports. I agreed to work for him.

He gave me a handsome cheque to cash. Part of the money was for me to procure a means of moving his container. He allocated an empty container loaded atop a trailer. I was to accompany the container to the hinterland of western Nigeria, where it would be loaded with teak wood from his sawmill. I was then to ensure that the loaded container arrived safely in Lagos, after which I would find a way through the bottlenecks of customs and excise so the shipment could be sent to India.

I remembered an acquaintance from my party days at the university in Zaria. He had worked in one of the banks in Zaria and risen to supervisor level. He later became involved in some unwholesome business, lost his job, and relocated to Lagos. He found me there, and since then I had been offering him continuous financial assistance. His wife had just put to bed, and he was jobless and broke.

I recruited him to help me locate a clearing and forwarding agent conversant with both ports in Lagos. He did. Through him, I was introduced to an Alhaji. I had now built a team of three people, including myself. I was set to ship wood to Asia and Europe—or so I thought.

To ensure the safe delivery of the wood enroute to Apapa Port in Lagos, I travelled sitting beside the trailer driver. On arrival around the port area, we encountered an unbelievable sea of containers mounted on trailers. There was a very long line of trailers, all struggling to gain access into the port. We were close to the tail end of the queue. I alighted from the trailer to go and locate my team.

I found both men at a small bar and food shop we had prearranged as our meeting point. That was where the bad news was broken to me. Nobody was allowed to ship wood outside Nigeria. The then military head of state and his cronies were the only ones moving wood out of the country. I could not believe my ears. From the moment I arrived from the hinterland into the port area, my cargo had begun to accumulate demurrage. A large chunk of money earmarked for the business was being lost by the minute.

After a week of reporting very early to the port every day and leaving late in the evening, I realized that it was indeed a fact: nobody, except the head of state and his cronies, was allowed to operate a wood export business. By now, a lot of money had been wasted on demurrage and other miscellaneous expenses.

There was a scramble to off-load the container and place it in a storage yard, as this was cheaper than leaving it on a trailer and continuing to incur losses. All the storage yards were already occupied. I had made the decision too late.

While roaming the area, a couple of men offered their help. I was sweet-talked into believing that an open space they were using for their business could be rented out to me. I was offered what sounded like a sweet deal. At that point, I was desperate to off-load the container. I just wanted it off the trailer. I accepted the deal and promptly paid the agreed fee. The container was off-loaded. As the trailer driver collected the balance of his fees, I felt a surge of relief pass through me—at least, no more demurrage payments.

I held a meeting with my team members. I instructed my friend, the former banker from Zaria, to keep all original copies of the documents pertaining to the container and its contents. I gave both men some money as payment for their efforts. Then I went home to my family.

All this while, my stress level had risen. I had someone else's money with me, a container full of teak wood, and I had been unsuccessful in shipping it out of Nigeria according to plan. I had spent a considerable sum paying demurrage. I felt it was time to take a break.

My wife and I agreed to take our two children to visit her parents. By now, her parents were papa and mama to us, and grandpa and grandma to our children.

After one week away from the stress of shipping wood, we returned to Lagos. As soon as I settled my family at home, I immediately boarded a bus to go and ascertain the condition of the container left at the roadside space operated by the men I had paid to watch over it.

As the bus passed the site, I looked out through the window. I sighted the men, but I did not see my container— or any container at all. I was utterly taken aback, confused, and worried.

I alighted from the bus further down the route, crossed over to the side where I had left my container, and approached the men seated on a bench. I spoke to them in their native language; they were all from northern Nigeria. I had felt confident leaving the container in their care because I spoke and understood their language, and they had assured me that the piece of land belonged to a former Inspector General of the Nigerian Police Force.

The men explained that a raid had taken place a few days after I left the container. The container had been towed to the compound of the local government council. They were unsure of its contents, and as such, it had been impounded. The men provided me with the contact of a lawyer who, they said, would be willing to help me retrieve my container from impound.

By now, I was smelling a rat. This had been the whole scheme from the outset. These men found desperate people who were tired of paying demurrage, lured them into believing they could store containers in their space for a small fee, and then alerted the local authorities to impound the containers. I had been suckered.

Desperate, I traced the location of the lawyer. He had an office tucked away in some kind of hideout. He offered to help, but his price was ridiculously high. We negotiated, and an agreement was reached. He demanded that I produce the original documents to prove ownership of the container. I would also need to make preparations to move the container away once it was released to me.

I went to inform my "boss." Understandably, he was angry. He had neither seen his goods nor heard from me in a week. Besides, I had spent a fair amount of the money allotted to me, with no results to show for it. He agreed that I should pay the lawyer, and he would meet me at the impound yard at the agreed time, with a trailer and a driver.

Next, I went to see my friend—the one in possession of the original documents proving ownership of the container. When I arrived at his home, he was not around. I met his wife nursing their newborn baby. I was touched by their condition and gave the baby a monetary gift. I then took my leave and went across the road to wait for my friend's return.

As soon as he walked into his house, I followed him closely. When he saw me, he looked at me in disbelief. I wondered why. I informed him of the latest development and explained that I needed the original documents in his possession in order to retrieve the container. He looked at me as if I had lost my mind. Then he asked, "Which original documents?" He continued, "Please, I do not know what you are talking about."

I tried to explain that we were supposed to ship a container of wood and that, because of demurrage, we had stored the container with some people. The container was now in a yard, impounded, and I needed the documents in his possession to retrieve it.

He looked at me in disbelief and said, "I do not know what you are talking about. I am not involved in any business with you, and I do not have any of your documents with me." I was shocked. His wife looked on in disbelief. I quietly took my leave.

On getting home, I related my experience to my wife, from the time I left the house to go and confirm whether the container was still where we had left it before travelling. She could not believe that any human being could be so diabolically cunning—lying with a bold face and being so outrightly deceptive. I had just seen another side of what people could turn into. I wondered if this was the kind of behavior that had cost him his career as a banker in Zaria.

The container was eventually retrieved from impound and handed back to its owner. Needless to say, he was totally unhappy with the turn of events. At the end of the day, nobody—except the head of state and his cronies—was moving wood exports out of Nigerian seaports. This was yet another of my attempts at a breakthrough, and it highlighted for me how dark the human heart can be, how full of evil it can become. What could have driven my "friend" to vehemently deny ever engaging in any business with me? Was it fear? Could he not have explained himself politely, without resorting to outright denial and disgusting lies? I chalked it up to lessons in extreme human behavior.

I not only lost a business opportunity—a good one at that—I also lost a benefactor, a man willing to go out on a limb to assist me when even my closest relatives were hiding their heads in the sand. That was the last time I ever came across him.

WAITING FOR A DOOR TO OPEN

At this time, life is looking bleak, future even bleaker, my two children are growing up fast, our son going on to fourteen and daughter going on to nine years old. Educational system in Nigeria at this time was totally up for sale, all kinds of private schools from kindergarten to universities were springing up in droves. These schools were also not cheap.

I began to contemplate my children's educational pursuit and the opportunities and options life in Nigeria portends for them, especially as we their parents are struggling to understand our situation economically. We were now relying on the services offered in our shop for sustenance. No further business opportunities or job prospects came my way.

It was in one of these days when I just stayed with my wife in the shop, hoping something will show up that a friend from Zaria dropped by, he has news for me that one of our Zaria friends has been looking for me for quite a while now. I remembered receiving this same message a couple of years back. I responded by saying I got such news before and went in search of him to no avail. He said to me, this time it is for real, he wants me to meet him at a wedding ceremony, he presented me with and invitation for the weeding.

On the weeding day, lo and behold my friend who has been looking for me was present as a guest in the weeding.

Our reunion was very pleasant, we talked animatedly and caught up on lost times. After the celebration, he offered me a ride home in his chauffer driven car. We both sat in the back seats and talked more. He was surprised that it has been a lot of struggles for me. He introduced me to providing commercial telephone services in our shop, cell phones were not accessible at that time in Nigeria. I asked if it was legal and he said it was legal, there were now private telephone carriers, unlike when only the federal government provided such services.

My friend promised to lend me the total amount I would need to purchase a telephone line from one of the private phone services providers.

At this time, my wife took our case to the spiritual realm. Even though we got married as Catholics, she decided to join the Mountain of Fire and Miracle Ministries—a fire-spitting church, one that believed we could pray ourselves out of captivity. I did not like it one bit. The fasting programs and prayer points were weird and frightening to me.

I almost tried to stop her, until she persuaded me to attend a revival where the church's general overseer was ministering. I attended, and my life changed. I learnt to fast and pray better. I began to read the Bible with spiritual understanding.

So, when I started keeping all appointments with my friend, with the intention of securing the loan, he was busy pursuing and sustaining his business. At the time, he was heavily mortgaged. He had purchased heavy-duty machinery for dredging and selling sharp sand. In a couple of years, he would own all the machinery and equipment, free of any lien.

At that point, however, he was constrained by cash flow. Still, I did not give up on keeping my appointments with him. He began to explain how his business was structured and shared his long-term goal of venturing into real estate— building and selling homes. My friend was smart and very business-savvy.

I intensified my prayers and fasting, that this opportunity would not go the way of the others—failing at the edge of materializing. My wife and I fasted and prayed together.

One day, my friend asked me to come to his home. I arrived as early as I could. He introduced me to his wife. That day, his wife wrote me a cheque for the full amount I had agreed upon with my friend as a loan. My friend later explained that he had to involve his wife, as he had no cash flow at the time—every inflow into his account was being directed toward the mortgage payments on his heavy-duty machinery and equipment.

On the day I received that cheque, it was the first breakthrough I could remember—after so many near-breakthroughs that failed at the very edge. It felt refreshingly different.

I went straight to a bank on the Island, cashed the cheque, and moved on to the best telephone company to make my purchase. I paid for the best phone system the company had at the time.

After the purchase, I ran home to drop off the phone, then went back to the shop to pay two years' rent. The landlord tried to discourage me. He told me that since he was reconstructing the building into a mini shopping complex, our shop would no longer have the vintage position facing the main road, where traffic was heavy. He said that if I insisted on keeping the shop, the plan was to reconstruct it facing an alleyway, and it would be smaller, for the same price. I agreed and went ahead to pay two years' rent.

He did not complete installing the shop door even three months after I had paid the rent. We secured the shop by locking the iron burglary-proof we had installed.

I remember the day we launched telephone services in our shop. The floor was still uncemented. There were no doors. A couple of cinder blocks lay inside. The shop was dusty. The sign writer could not meet the deadline—the two signs, written on white pieces of cloth, still had wet paint. I collected the signs and hoisted them at two strategic corners, pointing toward the alleyway where our shop now faced. My wife was busy sweeping the dusty floor and moving cement blocks around.

As soon as the signs went up, a few customers arrived, and the phone performed as if by magic. Numbers dialed went through, and conversations were clear. In the first hour of the first day, the revenue coming in was unbelievable. I immediately decided to cancel all outside appointments. Things were looking interesting.

My wife and I agreed not to touch the money from sales. We placed everything into a money bag. For household expenses, we spent what we already had at hand—no touching the business money. I opened an account for the business and made plans to pay off the loan. At the end of every month, I visited my friend, deposited the pre-agreed sum with his secretary, and collected receipts.

After five months, the total amount was paid off. Business was good.

Around this same time, my wife's sister was experiencing problems with her builder. She was constructing a house with four three-bedroom flats. The builder had spent a substantial amount of money crafting what he called a "German floor" foundation on a very solid piece of land, but his calculations were not adding up. When he reached lintel level and was about to proceed with the decking, I was drafted in to oversee the decking budget. I saved my sister-in-law a substantial amount of money.

When the decking was completed under my supervision, a significant quantity of cement remained. The excess cement was traded for already molded cement blocks, and the savings from iron rods were enough to encourage her to proceed with completing the second floor. I supervised the construction until the building was completed.

My reward was a promise: since my sister-in-law was immigrating with her family, she would introduce me to an immigration consultant once they had landed and settled in Canada. After settling her children there, she and her husband returned to live in Nigeria. I reminded her of her promise to introduce me to the consultant. She did so, albeit grudgingly. I began to sense that she feared she might have made a mistake in making that promise.

By this time, our telephone business had taken off, and business was booming. We decided to maintain a very low profile.

At the immigration consultant's office, I paid the required fees to obtain an application form. I completed the form and signed the necessary transfer of authority for the consultant to deal with the embassy on our behalf.

We submitted all the documentation required for immigration as economic migrants seeking permanent residency status. At that time, the Canadian embassy was located in Accra, Ghana. The waiting period after submission was approximately one year.

ALIVE BY MERCY ALONE

While we were waiting out the one-year period, my wife and I began contemplating building a permanent structure on our land. We owned a plot of land, which we had purchased during my teaching days.

Around the same time, my friend was asking that I stay close to him and observe his business. He suggested that we could go into real estate together once he had completed his payments and fully owned all his equipment and machinery. I was not sold on the idea. I was fed up with Nigeria. I had experienced nothing but disappointment at every turn, and now that I had this breakthrough, I was praying that the biggest of all breakthroughs would come to pass. I was no longer interested in attempting to survive in Nigeria.

I contacted a building contractor, who gave me a quotation for completing the foundation of a three-bedroom bungalow. I intended to put it up for rent and use the revenue to fund a new apartment we were planning to move into. I was not interested in living in the area where the plot of land was located.

I concluded an agreement with the building contractor on a Friday. On Saturday, my wife was at home doing house chores, while I was out paying bills, especially telephone bills. Our son was manning the telephone in the shop. While my wife and I were away from the shop, a call came through.

Our son picked up. An engineer left his phone number and asked that I come to see him in his office. There was a scheduled interview in Accra. That was how my son delivered the message to me.

I was beside myself with excitement and joy. I asked that we close the shop and join their mother at home. I explained the message to my wife, our son, and our daughter. My wife and I then began to educate both children on the virtue of being discreet and keeping important information to oneself. The news that their mother and I would be going to Accra for an interview at the Canadian embassy was, under no circumstances, to be mentioned anywhere. Our children understood and did exactly as we instructed.

I was presented with a letter of invitation to the interview by our consultant, who went by the prefix "Engineer." He arranged a briefing for all his clients who had been invited for interviews at the embassy.

My meeting with the building contractor later that day did not go well. I was not prepared to risk investing all the money we had saved on what was now looking like a "white elephant" project. Instead, we decided to keep the money aside for the building until the outcome of our interview was known. We had applied in April of the previous year and were invited for interview in March of the following year— an unprecedented eleven months.

Our story seemed to follow a pattern: just when we thought the worst was over, we were confronted with another unbelievable situation.

A group of us who had registered with the same consultant and were invited for interview attended a briefing in the consultant's conference room. A bundle of materials—compiled from debriefings of candidates who had previously attended similar interviews in Accra—was distributed to us. Much emphasis was placed on breaking our journey into segments before finally arriving in Accra, Ghana. We later discovered that this advice was a monumental mistake. Breaking the journey was a very poor idea.

Neither we nor our children disclosed that my wife and I were travelling to Accra. We invited my wife's younger brother to come over to babysit our son and daughter while we travelled for the interview. The children were very fond of their uncle.

On the morning of our planned journey to Accra, we woke up early. Our luggage was packed, instructions were given, and spending money was handed to the uncle to buy treats for the children.

Three of us set off to the bus stop to board the first of several buses, as outlined in the consultant's briefing.

My brother-in-law, my wife, and I got to the first intersection on our street when the lights went off—a total blackout, not uncommon. The blackout made us decide to take a more populated route to the bus stop. As we proceeded, the lights came back on. We continued on our way, excited and filled with joy at the new experience. My wife and I planned this to be a one-week getaway, as we had not had time to ourselves or taken a vacation since we got married. It was going to be exciting. We were also carrying a lot of money.

At the next intersection, with everywhere fully lit, we noticed a group of three individuals. We assumed they were returning from an all-night party. They behaved erratically, moved close to us, and demanded that we hand over everything in our possession.

At first, I thought they were joking, playing a prank. I was about to be tough with them until I saw one of them brandishing a shining stainless-steel gun, clearly ready to use it if necessary. My wife's bag was visible, and I shouted that all the money we had was in her bag. I did this as a decoy, to draw attention away from what I was carrying.

I had stashed a large portion of our money inside a toiletry bag, placed at the bottom of a shopping bag. On top of that was another shopping bag containing snacks, meant as a disguise. One of the hoodlums stayed close to me, refusing to let me make any move. I tried quietly to remove the bag containing the money and throw it into a dry drainage.

Whatever instinct or intuition the hoodlum had, he suddenly declared that the bulk of the money we were carrying was in my possession. He snatched the shopping bag and dashed away.

Our international passports—my wife's and mine—were also inside that bag. We had left our children's passports in our travel suitcase, thinking it would be easier to present only ours at the border. That suitcase was not touched; my wife's younger brother was carrying it. After emptying all the money from my wife's purse, the hoodlums handed it back to her.

The three men took off, excited that they had successfully completed their operation. We were left stunned and confused.

We returned home. After recounting our experience, some able-bodied men traced the route and chased after the robbers. We did not disclose our actual travel destination to our neighbors. I was determined to continue the journey and attend the interview.

I engaged the services of commercial motorcycle taxis, popularly called *okada*. First, I went to the bank to make a fresh withdrawal—we needed money. Then I visited the office of our immigration consultant. I was given photocopies of our recently stolen passports. At that point, I was grateful that we had engaged the services of a consultant; they meticulously kept records of their clients.

After collecting money from the bank and obtaining photocopies of documents from the consultant, I proceeded to the police station to lodge a complaint about the robbery and obtain a police report.

Before arriving at the police station, I consciously divided the money I had withdrawn from the bank. I placed one portion in my left pocket and another portion in the right pocket of my trousers.

At the police station desk, the desk officer listened to my complaint about the armed robbery carried out on us. He was particular about the time, the area, and the exact amount of money taken. I made it clear that my primary reason for reporting was to obtain a police report. I also wanted it officially recorded that documents bearing our identities had been stolen. We did not want our names associated with any crime, should those documents turn up in strange places.

The desk officer, however, seemed more interested in how much money had been taken from us. By this point, I was becoming exasperated. He noticed my frustration and sent me to the DPO's office, having taken my written statement.

At the DPO's office, the front-desk staff was operating a manual typewriter. She had a rude and condescending demeanor. I related our experience with the armed robbers earlier that morning. She was unmoved—disinterested and unsympathetic. She curtly informed me that I would need to pay a certain amount as the cost of procuring a police report.

At this point, the DPO briefly stepped out of his office, said nothing, and went back inside. His "front" stretched forth her hand, and I placed the stated amount in it.

After laying her paws on the money, she proceeded to type out a report, took it in to her boss for his signature, and returned with a signed copy of the police report. I collected it and headed back home.

On getting home, I found my wife in distress, confusion, and anxiety. She had picked up both clean and dirty laundry and was washing everything in sight. I was surprised and worried.

I then informed her that we had to get going before the day grew dark. We made a conscious decision to arrive in Accra two days before our scheduled interview. This later turned out to be a very wise decision.

We proceeded in the same manner we had started earlier, before the robbery incident. We were still following the consultant's briefing on how we should travel to Accra.

We arrived at the bus terminal where international travel to West African countries takes place. In hindsight, we should have boarded a vehicle heading directly to Accra. Instead, we split the journey—first boarding a bus to Cotonou, and then another from Cotonou to the Aflao border.

On arrival in Cotonou, we approached the currency exchange counters at the bus station to change our money into CFA francs and Ghanaian cedis. By the time we boarded the bus heading to Aflao, we were tired but grateful to be on our way.

I struck up a conversation with a Ghanaian man who spoke the language I had grown up speaking with my friends in Zaria. I found it amusing and familiar. I even bared my mind to him, thinking I was speaking to one of my childhood friends from Zaria. I told him about the armed robbery we had suffered earlier that day and that our passports had been stolen—information he would later use against us.

We arrived at the Aflao border late. All passengers alighted from the bus and walked toward the Ghana Immigration and Customs post. I asked my wife to walk in front of me as we moved briskly toward the officials.

Unknown to me, the Ghanaian man I had spoken with was right behind me, pointing a finger over my head and signaling to the officials to delay me.

I stole a glance behind me and noticed his gesture. It meant nothing to me at the time—until I was asked to step aside from the line of passengers being ushered through. My wife had already crossed over. I shouted after her to return.

I pleaded with the officials to let us go through. I presented the police report obtained earlier that day in Nigeria. From their demeanor, it was clear they were not adept at extorting money from people crossing into Ghana. They were timid, and that timidity almost cost us our lives. We were delayed until the border area was empty and it was very late into the night. They eventually demanded a paltry sum in cedis. I would have gladly given them much more.

When we were finally allowed through the border, we had to trek through dark stretches on our way to the Aflao bus terminal to board a bus to Accra, our final destination. Local money changers asked if we needed to exchange currency. We replied that we had all we needed, having already changed our money in Cotonou.

As we proceeded toward the bus terminal, a group of hoodlums appeared from nowhere. One of them came straight at me, holding a knife close to my stomach. They demanded that we hand over all our money or they would rip out my intestines. This time, all the money we had was in my wife's purse.

I did not realize it immediately, but my wife declared that over her "dead body" would they open my stomach. She held firmly to her purse and sprinted back toward the border post to report to the Ghanaian security. The security men promptly ran back with her. The hoodlums, realizing she had gone for help, left me and fled.

The Ghanaian security personnel arrested a few people who were lurking around and paraded them before us, but none of them were among those who had accosted us. They were released.

We were then escorted by the security officers until we arrived at the bus terminal. We thanked them profusely, and they returned to their post. The bus that was about to depart had space for only one more passenger. We were two.

We went on to board the next bus in line. We sat in the two front seats—my wife sat next to the driver, and I sat by the window on the passenger side. She was seated between the driver and me. We waited what felt like forever before the bus was full and ready to proceed to Accra.

As the journey progressed, I noticed my wife began singing Christian worship songs. As the night wore on, she sang a little louder. I asked her why she was singing so loudly. She retorted that it was because the driver was driving and sleeping. I told her, "You are the only one on this bus who sees everything. Please let me sleep—it has been a long day."

She replied, "You do not understand. Can't you see that the driver dozes off once in a while?" I insisted again that she was the only one noticing these things. I just wanted peace and quiet after all the unfortunate events since we embarked on the journey.

I soon dozed off.

Invariably, while I was asleep, the driver's dozing worsened to the point that my wife was forced to assist in controlling the steering—forcefully—alongside the driver. How she managed to do it, I do not know. She had never driven any vehicle, let alone maneuvered a bus full of sleeping passengers—mostly market women—with a sleeping driver.

Suddenly, I was wide awake. The driver was frantically pumping the brakes. A terrified group of market women were screaming and yelling obscenities in their native dialects, some cursing loudly. I shouted at them to keep quiet—that but for my wife, who had been making every effort, including singing loudly and even helping to keep the vehicle from veering into a ditch, we would all have been long gone.

The driver was pumping the brakes to avoid crashing into a broken-down trailer parked in the middle of the road, marked only by leaves and a pair of lanterns to indicate that a vehicle was on the highway, albeit disabled.

The driver eventually brought the bus under control. The market women began cheering and giving praise to God for delivering all of us from disaster—and possible death.

I wondered what kind of day we had lived through—from an armed robbery, to another robbery attempt with threats to rip out my innards, and now what could have been a ghastly vehicular accident. It was very scary, truly perplexing, and weird.

After the near accident, things seemed to calm down. We watched the day break as we passed through the industrial town of Tema, heading toward Accra. The sky was beautiful—blue-grey, with an orange moon still hanging. It was beautiful, perhaps an indication of the color that lay ahead, beautiful color.

We alighted from the bus in Accra and followed the directions provided in the consultant's briefing to a nearby hotel. The hotel was fully booked. The kind receptionist pointed us in the direction of another hotel not too far away.

We proceeded to the suggested hotel and were lucky to find a room available. We registered and paid, and were shown to our room. As we opened the door, luck began to shine on us. We were ushered into a very large room, with an air-conditioner working perfectly, and a bathroom and other amenities in top form. It was a great relief. We slept like babies. Thank God our appointment was not until the following day.

We eventually woke up to sunshine—a bright Accra mid-morning. We got ourselves ready to explore the city and get a feel of Accra. Our first port of call was a place serving local Nigerian delicacies. We ate to our delight, enjoying a very sumptuous meal. We felt much better, though still a little traumatized by the events of the past twenty-four hours. We were truly survivors.

After the meal, we called for a taxi. We noticed immediately that the taxis were neater and the drivers very polite. We asked to be taken to the Canadian embassy in

Accra, noting the time it took to get there, all in preparation for our interview the next day.

We enjoyed the services of our taxi driver and asked for a brief tour of Accra. When we returned to our hotel, we headed to a nearby police station, where there was a public telephone, to call home and check on how our children and their uncle were faring.

On our way to make the call, we noticed a very young girl—probably about six years old—walking home from school with a cell phone in her hand, speaking to someone, likely her parents. We were shocked. At that time, only the super-rich owned cell phones. You either had a landline or used a call center. Yet here in Accra was a six-year-old child with a phone.

We also observed the decorum around the police station—the cleanliness and the general ambience of the place.

After making our call home, we proceeded to a roadside food vendor and bought some barbecued beef, popularly called *suya*, with hot spice. We also bought some red wine packaged in cardboard boxes. This was the first time I had ever come across wine in cardboard boxes. We retired to our hotel room to eat dinner and continue our rest. We could not shake off the experiences of the last twenty-four hours; they lingered and lurked at the back of our minds.

The next morning, we were up early, dressed and ready for our interview at the Canadian embassy in Accra, Ghana. We were eerily calm. Our disposition was likely an after-effect of everything we had experienced since we embarked on the journey to Accra.

We boarded a taxi to the embassy. The embassy gate was free of touts and people with no business there. We were ushered into a waiting area—a kind of gazebo with circular seating—which allowed all interviewees a clear view of one another. Under normal circumstances, my wife and I might have found what was going on in that waiting area comical, but for the seriousness with which the participants carried out their "rituals."

Some interviewees clutched Bibles the size of the tablets on which Moses received the Ten Commandments. Others held Qur'ans, while some carried all kinds of religious literature. Everyone was engaged in some form of supplication—kneeling, crouching, or sitting on the bare floor. My wife and I simply sat, observing the unfolding drama with quiet composure.

A man noticed our calmness and could not help approaching us. He asked why we seemed so calm and unmoved by all the religiosity and drama around us. We calmly told him that we had passed through some very trying experiences getting to Accra. He shook his head and said quietly, "No wonder. Who would go through what you have and not become immune and indifferent?"

Indeed, we had become immune and indifferent to our surroundings and to all the drama playing out around us.

Soon, we heard our surname called and were ushered into another waiting area. There, we presented the original copies of our credentials. Photocopies had been submitted almost a year earlier, and these were now being verified against the originals. It was at this point that we submitted the police report and explained why we could not produce the original copies of our passports.

We knew our interview had gone well when the interviewer said to us, "I think you will be needing new passports. Welcome to Canada."

My wife jumped up from her seat, hugged me, and planted a beautiful kiss squarely on my lips. I was surreal—out of this world. I felt completely different, almost out of body, with a profound sense of freedom.

We thanked the interviewer profusely. He informed us that we should not have employed the services of an immigration consultant. He asked us to go and rest, and to return later in the day to pick up our visas. Four visas were issued—to my wife, myself, and our two children. We were now permanent residents of Canada. It was time to begin preparations for our journey to Canada.

Upon our return to Lagos, Nigeria, from Accra, Ghana, after the successful immigration interview, we made a conscious decision to hand our visas over to our immigration consultant. We did this for two reasons. First, we had already signed a letter authorizing him to collect documents on our behalf from the embassy, and we still owed him a balance for his services. We are honest people.

Second, about seven years earlier, we had been attacked by armed robbers. All the apartments in the compound where we lived were viciously ransacked. My family was fortunate to escape without injury, suffering only loss of property. Some of our neighbors were not so lucky.

We had not fully recovered from that midnight invasion, and now, with the recent attack on our way to Accra, we decided that our visas would be safer in the hands of our consultant until we were closer to leaving Nigeria.

Preparations included medical examinations for all four of us in the family—physical tests, submission of blood samples to a foreign hospital for analysis to rule out any contagious diseases, and all other required procedures. It also involved selling all our valuables to raise funds. At this period of our lives, we were a fasting and praying family, and the Almighty Lord showed up in our situation.

People were told that we were moving out of "town" to another "town" within Nigeria. That was our cover story, meant to prevent any gang-up or plans to rob us. News spread by word of mouth that we were selling land, business assets, and household property. Offers came in—much higher than what we would have asked for. We accepted them, and our funds built up quickly. We also had a considerable amount of money already saved.

A series of incidents occurred that I cannot help but include in my life story. I must have mentioned earlier that I once assisted my sister-in-law in completing the construction of four flats. While she was away on a trip abroad, she informed me that she would like to put the building up for sale and asked that I help locate a buyer. I found a young gentleman willing to make an offer and ready to pay in whatever currency she preferred. I conveyed this to her, and she said she would look into it.

Upon her return from the trip, on a Saturday afternoon, she invited me to accompany her to inspect the property. She was driving, and a few children joined us on the outing. During the drive, I reminded her that my buyer was willing to pay in U.S. dollars if she accepted his offer. I added humorously that I would like my commission to be paid in U.S. dollars as well.

I had never heard such a vicious response from her. She snapped, "What commission, and what U.S. dollars?" I was shocked. My mind began to race through all possible reasons for her reaction. I chose to remain quiet and let it pass. I consoled myself with the assurance from the buyer, who had already promised me, "Do not worry. If your 'sister' does not give you anything from the sale, once the deal is concluded, I will pay you."

While I am still on the issue of the sale of this property, I recall that the one time in my life I felt truly belittled and humiliated was as a result of searching for buyers for it. Although my sister-in-law had encouraged me to look for a buyer, she had also engaged the services of a realtor. I became aware of this development in a shocking and disgraceful manner.

One of the contacts I made—after she refused to accept the offer of the young man who had promised me a commission—introduced me to a relation of one of Nigeria's leaders, a gentleman who also worked for the presidency. He was in Lagos briefly, on a family visit, and was also sourcing property for personal business use. I was excited and eagerly led them to the property, which was quite far from where we were.

On arrival, my set of keys would not unlock the gate. To my horror, there was a large sign posted by a realtor—someone I had never seen or been informed about. I looked like a fraud. Not only did my keys fail, but there was clear evidence that the property had been placed in the hands of another agent without my knowledge.

I felt like a chicken drenched in water. Chills crawled up my spine. I was disgraced and ashamed. I have never felt so disrespected in my life. I have always avoided situations where I might be humiliated, and yet here I was.

We left the property quietly. Both men tried to console me. The prospective buyer said he believed my story and sympathized with my situation. He assured me that he did not think I had tried to deceive or defraud them. That was my only consolation.

Our medical results came back successful for all four of us. The sale of our land, business assets, and household property also went well. A good amount of money had been saved in the bank. We paid our consultant, retrieved our visas, purchased our flight tickets, and began sourcing foreign exchange.

BOXES OF DECEIT

In those days, securing foreign exchange at the best rates required strong connections with banks.

Those who promised to source for us reneged at the last minute. I remembered that my immediate elder sister's husband worked as a banker, and had serious "connections" in the bank. Yes, my sister and her husband who made me "homeless" in Lagos.

We reconciled our differences when information got to me a couple of years after our quarrel that she lost her brother-in-law, the last boy in her husband's family. He was serving NYSC, took ill briefly and passed on. I was close buddies with him, though he was younger than me.

The news shock me so badly that I forgot all the hurt caused me by this couple, I went to pay them a condolence visit, we thereafter got caught-up in our relationship.

Not quite after we resumed our relationship, my sister informed me her husband was into importation of some commodities for wholesale. I asked if her husband was a business man or a banker. She replied to me that he was still a banker, just branching out to make some more money. I warned that she should have informed her husband that people were being taken advantage of, then in Nigeria, that was the illicit business, obtaining under false pretenses.

The "business" her husband got into, "burnt" him and his family almost beyond recognition. The husband was introduced to importing commodities by one of his clients from the bank, his knowledge of the bank client's spoken language gave him false assurances. The client worked for a consortium of crooks and diabolic elements.

My sister's husband was not only duped of his life savings, he was drawn into the group's dark arts in an attempt to recoup his money, instead he fell more and more into debt, he was able to easily collect money from clients, friend, neighbors, and acquaintances He was neck deep into this torrid business with this consortium of crooks and diabolic elements.

At the height of this con job on my sister's husband, three huge metal boxes painted black with some kind of spotted red designs, painted light blue insides and a tiny rectangular two-inch by one-inch mirror placed in the middle of the inside cover of all three boxes. He was told to smuggle it into his bed room, he did. He actually placed it in a tiny closet like enclosure in his bedroom.

Whatever these charlatans told him, he must have believed that somehow those three huge boxes would eventually be filled with money. They remained empty. Somehow, his wife discovered the existence of the boxes. I do not know how she had not known earlier—after all, she sometimes shared the bedroom with her husband.

At the time, I was managing my own life with its ups and downs and struggles. I had managed to acquire a small vehicle, mainly to give my family some enjoyment. We had used it for picnics to the lagoon front, and on one such outing, I invited my sister's children to join us.

One eventful day, my sister visited me with stories of what her husband was going through and how their family had been left in tatters. She had just discovered that her husband was in possession of those three huge boxes. She told me she had contacted one of her husband's brothers, who lived in Lagos, to help remove the boxes from their bedroom for disposal. She was in tears, deeply sorrowful, her life unraveling piece by piece. I was moved by her distress and promised to join her husband's brother on the "rescue mission."

When I arrived, her husband was not around, nor was his brother. I found myself alone with my sister. The plan was that her husband should not know the boxes were being taken away—that once they were disposed of, he would be free from the grip of the con men. With my sister assisting, I loaded all three boxes into my van and drove them to my home. I offloaded them into a corner of our kitchen.

Everyone I thought might be willing to take the boxes wanted nothing to do with them. Before then, I had thought my life was hard—this turned out to be just the beginning of another stretch of bad luck. After transporting those boxes, the only successful trips my van made were to the mechanic's workshop. It drained my meagre resources, and I eventually sold the vehicle off at a giveaway price.

Yes, it was this same family I later turned to for help in finding connections to purchase foreign exchange. I am still surprised that I never asked my sister why she chose me to help dispose of her husband's diabolical boxes. Why me? I suppose all three of my sisters know that I love them dearly. I believe I love my sisters far more than they love me.

Even after all that my sister and her husband had done to me, I forgave them, resumed my relationship with them, and ended up carrying their "three boxes of horror."

In the end, I finally secured a connection at the bank and purchased a good sum of foreign exchange in travelers' cheques—Thomas Cook. To show my appreciation for the bank connection, I invited my sister and her husband to our house for breakfast. It was also an opportunity to formally inform them that we were relocating from Nigeria to Canada.

My sister never raised the issue of the mysterious boxes, nor did she mention my sacrifice in helping to remove them. She also never asked about the absence of her brother-in-law, who was supposed to be present during the evacuation of those boxes. At times, I wondered whether I had been deliberately deceived into removing those boxes on my own. I suppose I may never know.

At that time, owning personal computers, laptops, iPads, or even cell phones was still a distant dream in Nigeria. I began visiting what later came to be known as a cybercafé—places where one could browse the internet for an hourly fee and pay additional charges to print documents, with different rates for color or black-and-white prints.

I visited almost daily in the period leading up to our departure to Canada. I researched the various provinces and their child-friendly programs, as well as different cities. I eventually shortlisted a province and selected a city where we intended to land. I shared this decision with my wife.

In one of her many conversations with a female acquaintance, my wife mentioned the city. The woman asked whether we knew anyone there. The answer was no. She then informed my wife that her husband had a friend living in that very city, originally from Lagos, who had settled there with his family.

Her husband sent an email to his friend, asking whether he would be willing to assist us in settling down if we arrived in the city. The friend agreed. I only received this information a few days before our travel date. In a flurry of emails, I asked our new contact to help us secure accommodation. We did not want to settle for an apartment—we preferred to rent a house.

In my budget, I had allowed for six months of hotel accommodation, ideally one that would allow us to cook our meals. I had no idea how things worked and never imagined that securing rented accommodation would be so straightforward. Our contact and his family handled everything for us.

While in transit through Europe, we called our contact, not knowing how time zones worked. We called him at about 3:00 a.m. his time—very annoying. He was patient, explained the situation, and repeated his promise to be at the airport to receive us.

We eventually arrived at about 4:00 p.m. that same day. He was at the airport waiting for us. We somehow just knew he was the one, and he clearly identified us as well.

He drove us straight from the airport to his house, not too far away. We met his wife and their two very young children, a girl and a boy. We were offered refreshments—orange juice and water. After I had sipped some water, our host promptly informed me that further down the road was the accommodation he had negotiated for us, and that we needed to leave immediately to conclude the deal.

He drove a very short distance east on the same street where he lived, and there it was. I was excited, even though the house looked like it needed a fresh coat of paint and new carpets. He called the landlord. A young man arrived—the landlord—a student whose parents had purchased the house so he could earn rent money for his upkeep while in school.

Our host, an astute negotiator, convinced the landlord that the best tenants were new immigrants who did not yet know the tricks or games of landlord–tenant disputes. The landlord agreed, and we settled on a rent of eight hundred and fifty dollars per month, excluding utilities. I later learnt this was on the high side, but I did not mind. Within my first few hours in Canada, I now had an address and a postal code.

Our gracious host left the landlord and me to get acquainted as he rushed to the bank to withdraw one thousand dollars for me. At the time, I only had Thomas Cook travelers' cheques. Eight hundred and fifty dollars covered one month's rent, two hundred and fifty dollars was for purchasing bus pass booklets for two adults and two students, and the remainder was for miscellaneous expenses until we could open our own bank account. I was deeply appreciative of his thoughtfulness and kindness.

After securing and paying for the accommodation—a three-bedroom house with an unfinished basement—each of our children would have their own room. My wife and I would have a room to ourselves. All bedrooms were upstairs, with a living room, kitchen, and dining area downstairs.

LEARNING TO BELONG

We returned to our hosts' home, and I broke the good news to my family about the accommodation and the kindness shown to us. Dinner was served. After dinner, the two women huddled together, and our hostess patiently explained to my wife the process of obtaining a provincial healthcare card, a Social Insurance Number, and how and where to register the children for school. She wrote bus stop numbers on sticky notes and explained how to access the buses.

Her husband took me aside and explained where and how to obtain used furniture. He also told me that before anything else, I needed to activate our home phone.

We were shown to our room. I gathered my family together. We said our prayers and attempted to sleep. Sleep did not come easily—at least not for me. It was a combination of jet lag, the difference in time zones, and the excitement of having landed in Canada and securing accommodation for my family within the first hour of arrival. It was incredible.

We were up early the next morning. Our host led a quiet morning devotion on that beautiful Thursday. We ate breakfast prepared by our capable hostess. All four of us left the house and boarded a bus to the train station, requesting transfer tickets from the bus driver as instructed. With the transfers valid for ninety minutes on the public transit system, we followed the written directions given to us and headed downtown.

We completed the process of obtaining our healthcare cards and then proceeded to another government office to secure our Social Insurance Numbers. With these documents in hand, we felt Canadian—through and through.

The return journey came with a bit of drama. We were unsure which side of the bus stop to stand on for the ride back to our hosts' home. We stood on the wrong side while the correct bus made several trips in the opposite direction. It was not funny at the time. Eventually, we realized our mistake, crossed over, and boarded the right bus.

The children alighted at the bus stop closest to our hosts' home. We watched them ring the bell and enter the house. My wife and I stayed on the same bus and continued on to the bank. Thankfully, the bank operated late on Thursdays— a practice they still maintain to this day.

We arrived at the bank, where our assigned advisor was very welcoming and friendly. She told us that she, too, was an immigrant—she had emigrated from Sri Lanka. We opened a joint current account and a savings account. After converting our travelers' cheques into Canadian dollars, the bulk of the money was placed in savings, following her advice. She said we would need it as a down payment for the purchase of our first home, and she was right.

She asked if we needed cash, and we promptly requested enough to repay our host the one thousand dollars he had advanced us on arrival for rent, bus tickets, and miscellaneous expenses.

My wife and I will eternally be grateful for the financial advice we received that Thursday evening from our account advisor. I remember her saying, "Go out and take whatever job you can find. Do not wait for convenience. You must build a credit history. Credit history is built only through steady income and good references."

She promised to approve a credit card to help us begin building our credit history as soon as we started working and earning. She kept her promise.

Within twenty-four hours of touching down in Canada, we had an address, a postal code, a telephone number, two bank accounts, and a very sympathetic and knowledgeable financial advisor.

The next day was Friday. We informed our host and hostess that we would be leaving for our accommodation. They were very surprised—we had spent only two nights with them.

That Friday morning, my wife and our two children went to the city education board. Schools were assigned to the children according to their ages and our home address. From the board of education, my wife went straight to the allocated schools to complete the registration processes. School was to begin on Monday; fortunately, it was Thanksgiving Day in Canada, so the children resumed school on Tuesday.

My errand that Friday was to visit thrift stores to purchase furniture. For a fee, all purchases were delivered to our new address. Later that evening, we moved into our new home in Canada.

Our host and hostess had not anticipated that we would move into our own accommodation so quickly. They had already invited a few of their friends—Nigerians—for a barbecue on Sunday. Monday was a holiday, Thanksgiving Day. After church service, my family and I walked down to visit our hosts and their friends.

My wife and I were surprised when most of the guests asked questions about the newcomers who had just arrived and were staying with our hosts. They were astonished that we had settled into our own place within a couple of days. Many people, they said, would have overstayed their welcome, often leading to hosts and guests becoming sworn enemies. Different stories of such situations were shared at the barbecue.

My family and I were looked upon with admiration. We had spent only two nights; others might have milked the opportunity and overstayed their welcome. We did not.

After Thanksgiving Monday, the next day our children were off to school. Our host brought us an old computer from his place of work. It was a lifesaver. I could now draft résumés and search for jobs. The internet was slow in those days, but steady. About eight days after our arrival, I secured two starter jobs—one an hour's bus ride away, the other a half-hour ride.

We arrived in Canada at the beginning of fall. A week after Thanksgiving, I was already in the rat race of work. My day job was at an aluminum fabrication company. Extensible tents were built there to house U.S. military personnel and even Apache helicopters during Operation Desert Storm. My work was largely labor-intensive—measuring large aluminum beams, punching holes in them, and assembling and disassembling the structures for export to various destinations.

My evening job was project-based work in a laboratory. I went directly from my day job. The same bus that brought me from work passed right in front of our house. Most times, my wife would be at the window, hoping to catch a glimpse of me and wave. We did that every day, at the same time.

The laboratory work was seasonal. I was fortunate to have secured it, and it went a long way in strengthening my résumé. I was usually the last to leave, a few minutes to midnight. I would run to the bus stop to catch the bus that took me home—the race was for ten blocks. I dared not miss that bus.

I would clean up my workstation, lock up, and set the alarm in the laboratory, then begin the sprint to the bus stop to catch the last bus home. My wife was always awake, waiting for me. We would catch up on the day's events while I ate a very late dinner. Very early the next day, the same routine began again.

The children settled very well at school, made friends, and were happy to be in Canada.

THE LONG ROAD BACK TO JOY

Fortunately for us, winter did not arrive on time that year. We enjoyed an extended fall period. Then one morning, we woke up to snow. It was exhilarating—my first snow, our first snow. For the first time, I arrived late to work. My colleagues had a good laugh, and some joked that I probably thought the snow was anthrax, which was why I came in late. It was very funny.

My wife was job hunting, looking for any kind of work to earn some money as well. This did not happen immediately. Some evenings, she went job hunting with our son, both of them dropping off résumés at neighborhood stores and small businesses. At one point, she joked that her résumé ended up in garbage bins as soon as she turned her back.

There was a five-year gap between our son and his sister. She was now ten years old. So, when my wife discovered she was pregnant, we thought it was a joke. We had long given up on childbearing. The tension and stress back home had not provided a conducive atmosphere for her to conceive after our last child—not that we had not tried.

We broke the news to our two children. They were both very happy and excited to welcome an addition to the family. Later, the doctors told us it was a boy. Our daughter was especially pleased—she wanted to remain the only daughter in the family.

As the pregnancy progressed, we named the growing baby Philip, *Iteoluwakisi*. He was popular with all of us at home, and we simply called him Philip. He responded very well to his name.

While I was at work, whenever the children wanted to watch the only television in the living room downstairs, they would instruct Philip to kick their mother very hard. He always complied. When the kicks became unbearable, my wife would retire upstairs to our bedroom for the night. The children's trick always worked.

We all enjoyed speaking to Philip. After a while, we suspected he even recognized our individual voices.

We convinced my wife to suspend her job search, rest, relax, and give maximum attention to Philip. She did this very well. She often strolled through the malls after doctor's appointments, took long walks, ate well, and took good care of her growing baby.

I was at work one night. By then, I had my day job and a night job in a warehouse; the laboratory work was seasonal. Normally, my wife and I spoke during each of my breaks. That night, she told me she was upstairs in our room, the children were downstairs watching television, and Philip was fine.

It was a Friday night shift. The next day was Saturday, likely the day Philip would be delivered. The previous Wednesday had been my wife's last antenatal clinic visit. She and Philip were both certified healthy, and since Philip had grown to term, we were expecting delivery that weekend.

I arrived home early Saturday morning after my night shift and promptly passed out, sleeping deeply. I did not notice that my wife had quietly slipped out of our bed.

When I woke up, I noticed she was not in the room, and her car was not parked where it usually was. Panic set in. I assumed she must have noticed the signs of labor and gone to the hospital.

I rushed there. I found her car parked in the same spot where we usually parked during hospital visits. By the time I got to her, she was in induced labor—delivering a stillborn baby. Yes, we lost Philip.

In between the agony of delivering a stillborn child, she narrated what had happened. During our phone conversations the previous night while I was at work, she had noticed that Philip was not as active as usual. After a while, he became completely still. She assumed he was asleep. She did not want to raise a false alarm, pull me out of work, or plunge me into panic. Even when I returned home that morning, she remained considerate—wanting me to catch up on my rest.

To say the least, she went through hell delivering a stillborn baby naturally. It was excruciatingly painful, even with the steroid injection administered to her spinal cord.

Finally, Philip was delivered. He had a full head of hair, was tall, with long hands and feet, and slender fingers—a very handsome but lifeless child.

Our Philip, *Iteoluwakisi*, finally came to us—but without life. *Iteoluwakisi* means *the protection of the*

Almighty God does not shift. At that moment, it felt as though the protection of the Almighty over our family had shifted.

It was one of the saddest days of my life.

The hospitality, empathy, sympathy, and sense of community Canadians are known for were fully on display for our family during this trying time. Our baby, though not alive, was treated for a few hours as if he were. He was bathed, clothed, wrapped in swaddling clothes and soft blankets, and gently handed to my wife.

Grief counsellors were dispatched to attend to all of us, including the children. Discussions about funeral and burial arrangements began in earnest. We were reassured that we would not have to lift a finger—our only role was to indicate how we wished to proceed. Philip was left with us for several hours. We took turns carrying him in our arms, pouring out our souls to him, praying for him, and simply sharing the same space with him. After some hours, he was taken from us and later transported to the funeral home we had agreed upon.

My wife was eventually discharged from the hospital. When we returned home, in the days that followed, people we did not know began to stop by our door. Some rang the doorbell; most did not. These total strangers left flowers, greeting cards, and food items. It was deeply heartwarming and reaffirmed our belief in humanity. Truly, Canada is a great country.

I took time off work to grieve and to keep watch over my wife. We had never expected to be having children at this stage of our lives. The experience with Philip awakened in her a deep hunger and desire for another child—that was all she wanted.

I became afraid to leave her alone at home. With the help of one of her friends, who stayed with her and helped massage her body during recovery, we decided she should take up a job. She was introduced to an agency, and a job was secured for her. It involved driving to different locations, and it seemed workable. We needed something to occupy her mind, even if only briefly.

We both kept busy with our respective jobs, and I continued to pray that God would console her. At every opportunity, she insisted that she wanted another baby. We entered another phase of our lives. Almost every month, she would become pregnant, only to lose the pregnancy within weeks.

One such incident occurred while she was at work. She collapsed and was transported by ambulance to the hospital. I received a call at my workplace and was asked to remain on the phone with her as the ambulance rushed her to the emergency room.

After a while, we lost count of the miscarriages. We had tried for years in Nigeria—over ten years—and not once did she become pregnant. Yet in our first year in Canada, she was conceiving repeatedly. We marveled at it. Could it be the cold Canadian weather? The peace of mind? The reassuring environment and atmosphere? Whatever it was, life seemed to be restoring what had long been withheld.

Eighteen months after we landed in Canada, we moved into our own home. We purchased a lot directly from a home builder, chose a design suited to the land, and obtained a bank mortgage. Everything about our new home smelled clean, fresh, and new. By this time, I had stopped working two jobs. I was now employed in quality control at a Fortune 500 beverage production company.

Exactly thirty months to the day we lost Philip, we were blessed with the most precious little baby the world has ever seen. My wife did not want a repeat of the Philip experience. At the very first false alarm, she went straight to the hospital and vehemently refused to return home until she was delivered of her baby.

She was named Faith, because my wife and I held firmly to faith—that the desires of our hearts would be fulfilled, that we would be blessed with a child who would not only wipe away our tears but strengthen our family. Her brother loves her beyond words. Who would have thought that the sister who once wanted to remain the only girl in the family would so deeply adore her baby sister? She adores her completely.

Our prayer as parents—that our children would love and care for one another—is materializing right before our eyes.

Our first child, the elder brother to two sisters, is the quintessential firstborn: handsome, intelligent, calm, and deeply disciplined. His leadership among his sisters has been coordinated, loving, empathetic, and protective—worthy of emulation. Today, he is the proud father of a pair of amazing twin daughters, our little queens.

Our middle child, our first daughter, is known for her signature white teeth and dazzling smile—always joyful, always radiant. She is a very beautiful woman, one who could win any beauty pageant at any age. Her beauty is timeless. Growing up in Nigeria, she called herself "American Dumidu." Relatives later shortened it affectionately to "Dumama."

Our American Dumidu is now the mother of a very handsome boy—our first grandchild. His arrival brought a new flavor, a new meaning, and a fresh beginning to our family. It changed my wife and me from *mom and dad* to *grandma and grandpa*. The twins joyfully said *amen* to our new names.

Our last-born is now in her fourth year of college, studying physiology. She has always been fascinated by what goes on inside the human brain. Like all our children, we neither chose their course of study nor dictated their career paths. For this, we are deeply grateful to God—that all of them are university graduates and are walking their own chosen paths with confidence.

At the end of this year—December 28, to be precise— my wife and I will be celebrating forty years of marriage. This is no small feat. We have seen the highs and the lows of life together, and we have managed our marriage without recourse to outside help. I have never shared the inner workings of my home or marriage with anyone.

At the beginning of our relationship, I made a promise—to God, to myself, and to my wife—that I would marry only once. If it did not work, there would never be another marriage for me. I meant it. I worked daily to keep that promise, and my wife—*mom*—also respected it and worked just as hard to make our marriage succeed.

There is a saying that behind every successful man is a woman. Behind my success stands a beautiful, ageless woman with a soft, sweet voice—one who adores her man. Mom will not tolerate any form of disrespect directed at me from anyone—I mean *anyone* in this world. She has my back one hundred percent, and I have hers.

Now that we are empty nesters, we have chosen not to downsize. After our first home, we moved to a better part of the city and built a bigger, better home. These days, even though we each own a car, I still drive mom and myself to and from work, Monday through Friday. We pray together on our way to work and on our way back home. After work, we eat dinner and settle into the upstairs family room, glued to the television, content in each other's company. We look forward to retiring fully someday soon.

This sums up my story—from growing up in a small university town in Nigeria to becoming a grandfather in one of the best places to live in the world.

We arrived in Canada as a family of four—my wife and our two children. Along the way, we were blessed with another child.

Today, our children are raising children of their own, making us grandparents. Our prayer is that they too will live to see their children's children, and that one day, we will all gather around a table to celebrate Thanksgiving in Canada—

continuing our family tradition of prayer, gratitude, and feasting together as one big family.

"One of the truest tests of integrity is its blunt refusal to be compromised."

—Chinua Achebe

Acknowledgement

I am grateful to God Almighty for making it possible for me to write this book, depicting all the rough times growing up—my childhood, adulthood, and middle-age struggles in life. I clearly acknowledge that my faith in God is a very big contributing factor in my ability to chronicle my growing up in Zaria, Nigeria, and ending up as a Canadian.

I wish to thank my darling wife of over forty years, Angie Coker, for standing by me through thick and thin, literally. We have both passed through tougher times than easier ones. Her love, dedication, and belief in me are exceptional. Thank you very much, the love of my life.

My children, Kenneth, Felicia, and Faith, have shown me that, of a truth, children mirror their environment and learn from what surrounds them at home while growing up. My son Ken has been nothing less than the very best example of an elder brother to his two siblings; he has led the way for his sisters.

Felicia, my first daughter, is sheer beauty with a loving heart and a compassionate soul, and our last, Faith, is intelligent, scholarly, loving, kind, and filled with empathy.

My children, you have mirrored all the values your mom and I nurtured and encouraged in your lives. I thank you all for encouraging me to write this book.

I will also use this opportunity to thank all visitors and friends to our home in Canada who have listened to me as I regaled them with bits and pieces of my story from Zaria to

Calgary and were convinced that these stories were worth documenting in a book. You all kept asking me to do this; now the book is here. Thank you all very much.

I want to thank all of you who will read this book and relate to it as an example of resilience and faith in God. If you suspect that any part of this book mentions your involvement in my life, then this book is successful because of you. I say a very big thank you.

About The Author

I was born in the university town of Zaria in present day Kaduna State in Nigeria, West Africa.

My early years and up until I graduated from the prestigious Ahmadu bello university, Samaru Zaria were spent in Zaria.

I attended St. Georges Primary School, Sabon Gari Zaria for my early school learning and elementary school. I proceeded to St. Paul's College Wusasa, Zaria, after obtaining My First School living Certificate (FSLC) from St Georges Primary School in 1971.

I was admitted into the prestigious St. Paul's College modelled after Eton College UK, St Paul's like Eton is a boarding school for boys, with a rigorous tradition of discipline.

My university education was at the Ahmadu bello University, Samaru, Zaria, a first-generation Federal government University. I obtained a bachelor's degree with honors in chemistry. I my secondary school day's I was one of the very few science students who too Literature in English as a final year course.

In the university, I was a top member of the universities Student's Drama Society, a social club created for the purpose of interacting and providing entertainment through stage plays. It was a social club.

We acted and presented plays on all campuses of the university, our club was a very successful club, presented plays that were socially relevant at that time.

My most successful appearance was in a play, "the dilemma of a ghost" written by Ama Ata Aidoo was a Ghanaian author, poet, playwright, academic, and feminist, I played the part of Ato.

I was preparing for a stage play later in the night of November 30, 1979 when news arrived that my beloved mom had passed earlier that morning. Needless to say, I have never acted another play since.

I am married to my beloved wife of forty years, Angie and we are blessed with three children, Ken, Felicia and Faith, we also have three grandchildren, Caleb, Odion and Akhere.

I am most grateful for my family who have always been by me through thick and thin, and I am very appreciative of the opportunity to be a Canadian, one of the best things to have happened and shaped the later part of my life for good.